Media After
Deleuze

C
Subjec

DELEUZE ENCOUNTERS

Series Editor: Ian Buchanan, Professor and Director of the Institute for Social Transformation Research, University of Wollongong, Australia.

The *Deleuze Encounters* series provides students in philosophy and related subjects with concise and accessible introductions to the application of Deleuze's work in key areas of study. Each book demonstrates how Deleuze's ideas and concepts can enhance present work in a particular field.

Series titles include:

Cinema After Deleuze
Richard Rushton

Philosophy After Deleuze
Joe Hughes

Political Theory After Deleuze
Nathan Widder

Theology After Deleuze
Kristien Justaert

Feminist Theory After Deleuze
Kristien Justaert

ace After Deleuze
n Saldanha

c After Deleuze
d Campbell

Media After Deleuze

**TAUEL HARPER AND
DAVID SAVAT**

Bloomsbury Academic
An imprint of Bloomsbury Publishing Plc

B L O O M S B U R Y
LONDON · OXFORD · NEW YORK · NEW DELHI · SYDNEY

Bloomsbury Academic

An imprint of Bloomsbury Publishing Plc

50 Bedford Square	1385 Broadway
London	New York
WC1B 3DP	NY 10018
UK	USA

www.bloomsbury.com

Bloomsbury and the Diana logo are trademarks of Bloomsbury Publishing Plc

First published 2016

© Tauel Harper and David Savat, 2016

David Savat and Tauel Harper have asserted their right under the Copyright, Designs and Patents Act, 1988, to be identified as Authors of this work.

British Library Cataloguing-in-Publication Data
A catalogue record for this book is available from the British Library.

ISBN:	HB:	978-1-4725-3445-3
	PB:	978-1-4725-2490-4
	ePDF:	978-1-4411-0023-8
	ePub:	978-1-4725-2358-7

Library of Congress Cataloging-in-Publication Data
A catalogue record for this book is available from the Library of Congress.

Series: Deleuze Encounters

Typeset by Fakenham Prepress Solutions, Fakenham, Norfolk NR21 8NN
Printed and bound in Great Britain

To Jaak Savat – pages 129 and 161 are for you –
keep tinkering away.

CONTENTS

ACKNOWLEDGEMENTS

This book has been inspired by a large number of people, including friends, colleagues and students who forced us to think through our ideas on Deleuze, Guattari and media. In particular it is our engagement with our students at both undergraduate and postgraduate level that helped us clarify ideas. A special thank you goes to Sian Tomkinson, Colleen Harmer, Emma Nicoletti, Christina Chau and Michael Blanchard. Their engagement with Deleuze and Guattari has deepened our own understanding of their work. It is our great pleasure to have worked with such intrepid and passionate thinkers.

We would also like to thank Ian Cook and Greg Thompson at Murdoch University. The discussions we've had over the years were most helpful in thinking through our ideas. We are also grateful for the opportunities we've had to discuss this work with our colleagues at the University of Western Australia.

We would like to take the opportunity to thank the team at Bloomsbury Publishing for their most welcome patience and support in bringing this project to publication. We would particularly like to thank Liza Thompson and Frankie Mace for their patience and support. Our thanks also go to Kim Storry, Jill Morris and Ken Bruce for their assistance in editing the book. Thanks also go to Gail Harper for her assistance with indexing the final proofs.

This book would not have been possible without the generosity and guidance of Ian Buchanan, whose questioning over the years has been of great help. We also thank the Institute for Social Transformation Research (ISTR) at the University of Wollongong, and especially The Schizoanalytic Applications Research Collective (SARC) for the opportunity to present our work. An outlandish presentation at one particular SARC symposium significantly intensified and extended our thinking on the Body without Organs – with the state of academia today, especially with its increased bureaucratisation and corporatisation, such moments of deterritorialisation are increasingly too far and few between.

Thanks also go to the broader community of scholars engaging with the work of both Deleuze and Guattari. At the various conferences where we encountered each other, they always formed an inclusive, warm and intellectually rigorous group, fostering different ways of thinking about a problem. In particular the Amsterdam, Lisbon and Istanbul conferences fostered many of the ideas and challenges contained in these pages.

Finally, we would like to thank our families and partners. This book was written during a time of very intense deterritorialisation and we could not have remained grounded without the support, love and inspiration of these wonderful people. We are forever grateful.

INTRODUCTION

Violence on television only affects children whose parents act like television personalities.

LINER NOTE FOR THE ALBUM *STOP MAKING SENSE* BY TALKING HEADS (1984)

Deleuze wrote a lot about a variety of media throughout his work, ranging from his engagement with cinema to literature, painting and music. This book is an attempt to examine media using the innovative concepts provided by Deleuze, as well as his frequent co-author Guattari. This is no small task, as both Deleuze and Guattari wrote extensively about media, both directly and indirectly. While in much of their work they point to the productive, and often positive, power of media, they often contrast this with the negative effects of mass media. They understand much of mass media, and their precursor public communication, as inherently repressive, indoctrinating and reactionary. Their argument comes from the idea that things that 'mediate' – be they representations, languages or systems of senders, wires and receivers – tend to impose a level of homogenisation and control over the way we engage with the world. Deleuze's philosophy, along with Guattari's, values the different, the contingent and the local, whereas mass mediation tends to imply the general, the transcendental and the global. Where media studies has tended to seek to establish general rules of media effects, audience behaviour, news framing, strategic communication and genre, Deleuze begins his philosophy with the notion that the general rule is always a poorly conceived and dangerous thing. He argues that all social formations need to be assessed in light of the kind of connections they form, the way they harness our desire and, most importantly, what they produce at a local and immanent level. Thinking about the media out of the context of the immanent social and psychological formations the media 'plugs into' can only work to re-institutionalise a philosophy of the general. This kind of thinking is unsuited to contemporary media research and is what this book attempts to avoid.

We wanted to write this book because there seems to be more need than ever for a toolkit of concepts that can be used to understand media at an immanent level. We want to move away from notions of what everyone does, what everyone thinks and how everyone understands and toward a more focused analysis of how media – however expansive and general – produce affects at the local level. We have noticed that our students are more than ready to accept that the old 'transcendental' regimes of signs and mediation are no longer relevant. In the world of digital media the traditional binaries of media studies such as broadcast/narrowcast, signifier/ signified, real/virtual and producer/audience have been rendered obsolete. A social media message board does not fit nicely with any of these binaries or concepts. The audience is simultaneously the producer and the number of either category and is as much determined by the content of the message as the form it appears in; the virtual is not opposed to the real, rather it produces the real, while signifiers don't refer to a transcendent reality but function directly to produce an 'affect'. Deleuze, particularly through his work with Guattari, provides a conceptual toolkit designed specifically for this brave new world. As they say at the beginning of *A Thousand Plateaus*, 'there is no longer a tripartite division between a field of reality (the world) and a field of representation (the book) and a field of subjectivity (the author)' (Deleuze and Guattari 2004b, 25). Instead, we have a world composed of connections, flows of desire and effects that are simultaneously imprinted on the subject, the media and reality.

It is not just a happy coincidence that Deleuze and Guattari came up with a broad and useful set of concepts to analyse contemporary media. In their work together they develop a conceptual toolkit that they suggest could be applied to any particular situation, as long as those tools are applied in an itinerant and ad hoc manner. There are some central themes that pervade all of Deleuze and Guattari's work, which we will outline shortly; however, the overriding rule is that *rules in general* are some of the most dangerous things of all. Any transcendental use of rules, meaning the assumption that a rule is perfect, correct and true at all times, at all points, is likely to override the different and the immanent and actually ends up being wrong after all. It is within this double bind that we find Deleuze and Guattari's work to be both challenging and rewarding – the plasticity of their concepts means that it is possible to apply their ideas to anything, including media; however, the refusal to establish transcendental definitions for those concepts means that there are many opportunities for different interpretations and applications to flourish. This is one of the reasons that so much work on Deleuze's oeuvre tends to present itself as a 'how to', 'beginners' guide' or 'introduction to', as every perspective on the incredibly rich set of concepts Deleuze and Guattari present brings out something new in them. While many such differences emerge within this book, it is our hope that we have managed to make the differences themselves become productive.

Concrete rules and abstract machines

Deleuze and Guattari themselves are famous for using different words to refer to the same concepts, both between and within texts (Hughes 2012); in an attempt to avoid the dangers of representation, they are continually coming up with new words for things and new ways to present their ideas. This clearly makes it difficult to write about Deleuzean ideas in consistent language, so in order to assist the unfamiliar reader we shall use this introduction to establish a few of the 'concrete rules and abstract machines' that pervade Deleuze's work – a few of the concepts and ideas that run throughout both Deleuze's as well as Guattari's work and throughout this book – and thus come to constitute a guide to understanding media after Deleuze.

The first of these is the importance of the concept of difference in the work of Deleuze and Guattari. Difference is important because it consistently comes up with disagreements with 'what is' so that the new can emerge. This is an idea that emerged in Deleuze's work, particularly in *Difference and Repetition* (Deleuze 2004b) and *Proust and Signs* (Deleuze 2008), well before he met with Guattari. Deleuze locates 'difference' as underlying the source of thought itself. It is, he argues, when we fail to reconcile what we already know, remember or expect with what we encounter that we are forced to come up with new ways of thinking. Simply put, the representation of a thing never equates to the thing itself, and it is the difference between the two that sets thought in motion (Deleuze 2008, 101). Without such difference, thinking and creativity would wither away. Similarly, Guattari highlights the importance of difference in his own work, specifically through the concept of 'a-signifying ruptures' – eruptions of difference that can begin something new (Guattari 1989, 136). It is no surprise to find that their work together is focused on valuing difference, on trying to construct forms of analysis and engagement that pay attention to the detail, the local and the immanent. It is interesting to note that Deleuze and Guattari each had different methods of appreciating difference. Guattari travelled widely and revelled in the immersion in difference he found in cultures as diverse as Brazil and Japan; on the other hand, Deleuze preferred not to travel anywhere at all and instead revelled in the differences that became apparent through his own personal repetitions, returning to the same places, returning to the same tunes, but always finding them different. Together, they assure us that difference is the actual; the world is eminently and unavoidably different, through time, movement and perception; a tree at six in the morning is not the same thing as that tree at noon; the tree being felled is not the same as the tree being climbed; the tree I am thinking of is not the same as the tree you are thinking of. Difference is everywhere – it is the inevitable and productive nature of existence.

The next general theme is the danger involved in the transcendental: that is, 'ideals', representations and generalisations. This is the flip side of appreciating difference – understanding that transcendental ideals tend to override that difference and impose not just conformity but, also, an inattention to the local and unique detail. Stated differently, representational models of thought, or what they refer to as arborescent ways of thinking, are incapable of recognising and understanding difference, multiplicity (Deleuze and Guattari 1987, 6). This is one of Deleuze and Guattari's clearest concerns about the effect of media and communication on our world – that the transcendental elements of media are isolated, repeated, deified and then spread all over the world in one homogeneous imprint, effectively overriding differences everywhere. This is not simply about the problems of cultural imperialism – that supermodels inspire anorexia across the globe – but also (and at the same time) it is about the spread of a singular world view (capitalism) and a single psychiatric diagnosis (Oedipal lack).

> What is produced by capitalistic subjectivity, what comes to us through the media, the family, and all the resources that surround us, is not just ideas; it is not just the transmission of meanings through signifying statements; nor is it models of identity, or identifications with maternal and paternal poles, and so on. More essentially, it is systems of direct connection between, on the one hand, the great machines of production and social control and, on the other, psychic agencies, the way of perceiving the world. (Guattari and Rolnik 2008, 91)

This is the problem that Deleuze and Guattari spell out in their first book together, *Anti-Oedipus*, volume one of *Capitalism and Schizophrenia*. They attack Freud's location of all desire as stemming from lack – specifically familial, sexual lack (lack of the opposite sex parent, lack of a penis) – which they view as an inherently negative formulation. Freud also made the mistake of assuming that what may have been true for some of his patients was not necessarily true for all of them; he understood that there was a relationship between the unconscious and the social, but then assumed that all unconsciousness and all societies must be the same. This Freudian analysis then became a formulaic doctrine used to diagnose all psychiatric disorders, no matter how inappropriate the 'general rule' Freud created was for the specific circumstances being analysed. Why, ask Deleuze and Guattari, does Freud gravitate towards his transcendental rules, which repress difference, while ignoring the immanent situations, conditions and possibilities that 'might have made his discoveries genuinely liberatory instead of sadly imprisoning' (Buchanan 2000, 23–4)? The answer to this question is that Freud's entire field of action and conditions of possibility – the belief in the saviour, the profusion of lack, the construction of an isolated individual and the faith in the transcendental – are as much a part of 'the great machines of production and social control' as his diagnoses. Here Deleuze and Guattari's key move is that, while they accept Freud's model of the unconscious, they reverse that model, and specifically the manner in which repression functions (Bell 2012, 136): 'The unconscious does not apply pressure to consciousness; rather, consciousness applies pressure and strait-jackets the unconscious, to prevent its escape' (2012, 338). In this way, they situate the unconscious, what they refer to as desire, in the opposite way to Freud – desire creates the social field. As part of that move they similarly adopt Marx's approach to capitalism but connect desire to the productions of the political economy. In this way, they link the political economy and the libidinal economy to develop a general theory of society as a general theory of flows (Deleuze and Guattari 1983, 262).

This brings us on to the next general theme, which is the concept of the assemblage, or the notion that nothing exists in isolation but is always forming a part of a particular machine.

> The breast is a machine that produces milk, and the mouth is a machine coupled to it. The mouth of the anorexic wavers between several functions; its possessor is uncertain as to whether it is an eating machine, an anal machine, a talking machine or a breathing machine. (Deleuze and Guattari 2004a, 1)

Everything, Deleuze and Guattari argue, is a machine of a machine – nothing exists in isolation, but is brought together by connections and flows (Deleuze and Guattari 2004a, 39). The concept of the assemblage is used to articulate the point that you cannot view things in isolation – things are always connected and are always making connections. For instance, you can't just view the internet as a thing in and of itself, but only in terms of the assemblages it forms a part of. At any point the internet forms multiple different assemblages and its 'nature' changes according to the assemblage it forms. The internet functions in one way as a machine when it is plugged into a pedagogical assemblage by the teacher looking for resources. It functions in a completely different way as a machine when it is plugged into an erotic assemblage, even if it is the exact same teacher looking for resources. To be certain, the mechanisms of the assemblages do determine what function they play independently: in both cases the internet is the machinic part of the assemblage used for searching and appraising. However, the machine as a whole changes completely – in its form, its content, its composition and its products – according to which assemblage it is connected to. The only thing holding the machine together is the fact that it is able to make a connection, channel a flow and become productive. The moment that process stops, the machine falls apart, to be replaced by new connections, new machines.

Deleuze and Guattari go to extreme lengths to try to spell out that we are always engaged as part of a particular assemblage, as well as constituted as subjects in that process of assembly. There is a constant arrangement or arranging in process.[1] We are never actually isolated, cut off, alone, but always parts of larger machines. One of the ways this manifests is in their use of the term 'affect', which they use as a noun to refer to the change brought about by being connected to an assemblage. It is important to note that by affect Deleuze and Guattari are not referring to personal feelings or anything about the individual; they are referring to a change of intensity within an assemblage. As the chapter on image machines in this book explains, whereas a feeling is an experience that has been checked against memory and knowledge and then given a name, an affect is an unconscious change in intensity that doesn't exist as an articulation but rather exists in the way it changes the potential of the assemblage (Shouse 2005). Media studies has long been preoccupied with media effects – that is, how behaviour is changed by the viewing of media – whereas Deleuze and Guattari's approach is to think about media in terms of 'affects': that is, how the media machines we engage with change our unconscious thinking patterns, shift our intensities and thus alter the domain of our possible actions. This sort of effect

> crosses the threshold of a new kind of perception, one that is below or above the human. This new perception is multiple and anarchic, nonintentional and asubjective; it is no longer subordinated to the requirements of representation and idealisation, recognition and designation. It is affirmed before the intervention of concepts, and without the limitations of the fixed human eye. (Shaviro 1993, 31)

The difference between an effect, viewed as behavioural change because of viewing media, and affect, seen as change in intensity from connecting to an assemblage, is that the former focuses upon representations and discrete events while the latter focuses on relationships, experiences and flows. Affects only arise as a result of specific connections, and these connections are inherently subjective. Guattari, for his part, argues that these sorts of affective connections proliferate through the unconscious to create a 'machinic assemblage' of the psyche that we take everywhere, proliferating affects as we go. A change in the environment produces an affect upon the psyche, which produces an affect upon the social; thus these unconscious affects shape everything we encounter. Media analysis founders when it focuses on effects, as if a particular isolated sign produced an identifiable feeling and caused a resultant behaviour – that kind of gross generalisation is exactly what Deleuze and Guattari are working against. Instead, we should consider the affect – that is, 'attraction and repulsion as we directly experience them on our nerve-endings' (Powell 2002, 66) – and think about what that tells us about the assemblages we're forming; we should not make the mistake of thinking that the representation itself is a cause – the representation is a symptom. Do not think about media in terms of what they represent; think about media in terms of what they produce.

The final key theme in Deleuze and Guattari's work is the importance of desire, which they locate at the heart of all production. Deleuze and Guattari call desire 'desiring-production' in order to distance their conception of desire from Freud and bring it closer to Marx's theory of productive force determinism. Desire creates the world we inhabit:

> *social production is purely and simply desiring-production itself under determinate conditions.* We maintain that the social field is immediately invested by desire, that it is the historically determined product of desire, and that libido has no need of any mediation or sublimation, any psychic operation, any transformation, in order to invade and invest the productive forces and the relations of production. *There is only desire and the social, and nothing else.* (Deleuze and Guattari 2004a, 31 [original emphasis])

This formulation of desiring-production resists the Freudian and Lacanian constructions of desire as arising from lack – that we want because we don't have. Instead, Deleuze and Guattari site desire as a fundamental force of production – everything that has life energy produces and, at the same time, every investment of desire is productive. Our desire flows in an effort to produce and, as it flows, it forms connections, which give rise to assemblages, which distribute its affect. Desiring-production – the flow of desire through, or rather, as assemblages, as assembly or a constant arranging – produces the world we know. Aside from challenging the transcendental nature of the lack that Freud imagines, this position argues that the world we have is, essentially, the world we desire. Yet, clearly, it isn't perfect, and there lies the rub. How is it that our desires have managed to produce this world that nevertheless keeps us quite unhappy? Why do we continue to form assemblages and produce affects that give rise to crises after crises, keeping us in a constant neurotic state (Guattari and Rolnik 2008, 15–16)? The digital assemblage makes the productive nature of desire all the more apparent – your desire to engage with friends on social media produces an advertising market, a social graph and a trail of consumer data thousands of items long, all of which can be used to generate production and none of which needs to manifest a physical product. Here your desire has been made to work by an assemblage that has captured your desire to connect, and invested it in an assemblage of consumption. Looking at media after Deleuze, we need to ask ourselves why, given the multiple, itinerant and immanent nature of desire, do we all end up desiring the same things? What perversion of desire has taken place to make us produce the world that we do? It is our hope that this book helps to answer some of these questions.

A note on structure

We intend this book to be read by media studies scholars who are wondering how they can update their conceptual toolkit in light of the work of Deleuze and Guattari. As such, we've tended to present each chapter as an investigation of one of the central concerns of traditional media studies through the lens of Deleuzean concepts. As Deleuze and Guattari suggest with *A Thousand Plateaus*, you should feel free to read the chapters in any order you wish; any chapter 'can be connected to anything other, and must be' (Deleuze and Guattari 2004b, 7). We started with the idea that we would cover machines as technologies first, that is, in their operation as more concrete machines, and then to explore more 'abstract' machines in the latter parts of the book. However, such a distinction is quite problematic, as Deleuze and Guattari's concept of the assemblage very quickly makes clear. Thought, the world, cannot be neatly separated in this way. This is precisely why they ask us to reject representational models of thought, to reject the trees growing in our heads, reject filiation, and instead adopt the rhizome as a model, which operates through alliance – always another connection, always in the middle, 'and ... and ... and ...', as they state (1987, 25). We explore these ideas in the context of the assemblage in the following chapter, but the point here is that they urge us to avoid questions of the 'what does this mean', 'where do I come from' type and instead provoke us to ask how something works. So, the first chapter investigates the notion of media as an assemblage. It seeks to outline how the assemblage can be understood as a concept for media analysis as well as presenting some of the arguments Deleuze and Guattari make about how assemblages also produce subjectivities; as the (media) assemblage of the international world, capitalism has produced the consumer as the ideal subject.

The second chapter deals with images and here is where we engage more specifically with the notion of affect. Images are the perfect medium for affect because they have a clear, sensational, effect on us, and it is only after the fact that we can try to explain or represent that sensation. In this chapter we also examine the operation of what Deleuze and Guattari refer to as the abstract machine of faciality, which they locate as a key machine in the mass production of subjectivity in capitalism. Faciality, Deleuze and Guattari's term for the interface of assemblages, is the point at which affect is expressed, related and 'fed into' another machine.

The operation, or rather production, of culture is explored in more detail in the third chapter, 'Distribution machines'. Here we examine media in terms of their connections, structures and distributions. Deleuze and Guattari famously discuss the relative strengths of rhizomes and trees as distributive structures and such structures can be found throughout media, with the internet in some ways operating as a model for a rhizome, while a newspaper tends to reflect the arborescent nature of a tree, though even that distinction is a very dubious one to draw, because the internet as it turns out is also a very nice place to grow trees. In this way we show that these distinctions are far from simple, as well as try to highlight the problems and potentials of each type of distribution machine.

In the fourth chapter, 'Play and games', we discuss how play emerges from the desire to connect and how games create an assemblage to maintain the flow of that desire. The chapter contains a couple of different Deleuzean concepts with which to critique games, beginning with smooth and striated space and then progressing to the legitimate and illegitimate syntheses of desiring-production. The game chapter really focuses on how media assemblages can harness and inscribe our desire.

The chapter 'News and information media' discusses the changing assemblage of information media given the decline of the centralised public sphere. It raises the question of what distinguishes a flow of news from a flow of advertising and uses Deleuze and Guattari's concept of the 'Body without Organs' to establish the sort of organising principle needed to produce news from desire. In an effort to account for the rise of citizen journalism, the chapter also contrasts state news to nomad news: the former being imperial and hegemonic, the later itinerant and minor.

In the chapter titled 'Advertising' we take a closer look at desire and the difference between desire as conceived by Freud and desiring-production as conceived by Deleuze and Guattari. To do this, we recount Freud's transcendental application of the Oedipal myth and draw some of the lines that Deleuze and Guattari connect between capitalism, lack and Oedipal thought. We then discuss how advertising thrives on the construction of desire as lack, while also considering some of the contemporary advertising techniques that thrive on the productivity of desire.

In the final chapter 'Media content and audiences: Genre, difference and repetition' we examine the creation of media tropes and genres by media assemblages. This provides us with a chance to more fully explore the original points Deleuze makes about difference and repetition throughout his work. By examining the creation of genre and tropes in the world of big data audience analysis we use this chapter to articulate what needs to be done to achieve true creativity in the world of absolutely massified media.

As mentioned at the beginning of this chapter, dealing with Deleuze, Guattari and media is no easy task. It will be obvious in reading this book that we have employed both Deleuze's own work and his collaborative work with Guattari, as well as Guattari's own work. Their work, including Deleuze's own, has at its core a political impetus, a critique of individualism, which some work on Deleuze sometimes loses sight of. Indeed, the key idea of *Anti-Oedipus*, which persists throughout both Deleuze's and Guattari's work, is that 'the unconscious is directly related to a whole social field, both economic and political, rather than the mythical and familial grid traditionally employed by psycho-analysis' (Deleuze 2004c, 194). In this way we see no need to somehow 'extract' Guattari from Deleuze, and in fact view this as dangerous, as Wallin makes clear when he refers to Guattari's 'dubious disappearance' in contemporary philosophical debates (Wallin 2012, 148). There is also the key point that Guattari was in some respects even more engaged than Deleuze in thinking about the problems, and the creative potential, associated with different media, including with respect to his ideas around the need for a transition to what he termed a 'post-media age'.

We have also tried to ensure that this is a book that any media studies student can understand – that it takes some central concerns of the discipline, such as technological determinism, media effects and marketing, and examines them in a way that illuminates not only what Deleuze and Guattari might have to say about these issues but, also how we might use their conceptual toolkit to assess these topics in an innovative way. Breaking down Deleuze and Guattari's strange and changeable theoretical vocab-ulary to everyday language has been a challenge and in writing a book such as this there is no doubt that we have obscured a lot of the differences and potentials that might unfold from their work. Sometimes deliberately, sometimes accidentally, we have closed off particular lines of flight. Given the relatively expansive engagement with Deleuze in the area of cinema and film studies, we have quite deliberately focused less on Deleuze's *Cinema* books, for example. There are enough texts, for a variety of readers, that engage with Deleuze's work on cinema in better ways than we could do here. From this perspective there will no doubt be people who will admonish us for focusing less on music, or some other aspect or form of media. Certainly, we could have spent more time on so-called digital media, especially in the context of the wide uptake of Deleuze's essay on 'the control society' it assembles. This is not at all to state that we do not engage with film, music or digital media, but that these are not intended to be sole or major focal points in and of themselves. This is in part the point of this book

– that it's important to take a more general, broader view of media through Deleuze and Guattari's work.

We believe that Deleuze and Guattari understand the production of mass commodity culture, with its celebration and affirmation of individuality, as the most significant problem confronting the world. In our world it is near impossible to somehow extract or separate us from 'our' media – even something as innocuously simple as handwriting is productive of what so many think it means to be 'human' (Ong 2000). In this respect, digital media precisely problematise our older distinctions of media (Maras 2000). This is why we need Deleuze, as well as Guattari. Their work, and especially their collaborative work, is well placed to provide a more general analysis of the flows of production that are constituted by media. A critique of that production, in which so much of what is 'media' is involved, is at the core of their work. In short, this book presents only fragments of Deleuze's and Guattari's ideas, and they are highly imperfect fragments at that. We are sure the book will produce more questions than answers about media after Deleuze and Guattari. Luckily, that's exactly what they would have wanted.

CHAPTER ONE

Assemblages

The rationality, the efficiency, of an assemblage does not exist without the passions the assemblage brings into play, without the desires that constitute it as much as it constitutes them.

(DELEUZE AND GUATTARI 1987, 399)

Desire is not form, but a procedure, a process.

(DELEUZE AND GUATTARI 1986, 8)

The word media is used in a variety of different ways. Adding to the confusion is that the word can be the same in both its plural and singular use (Maras 2000). Key to many of its uses, though, is the notion that it refers to something that is in the middle, that it serves as some point, layer or substance; that it connects as well as cultivates or can function as an environment in some way. It is partly for this reason that Marshall McLuhan initially favoured the statement 'the medium is the massage' rather than the 'medium is the message' as the title of one of his books. Given he made choices such as this, it is clear that there are interesting connections between Deleuze's work and that of McLuhan. As Peter Zhang (2011) has argued, Deleuze made use of a number of McLuhan's ideas, picking them up and building new conceptual assemblages. Indeed, for Deleuze, McLuhan was an important mediator (Theall 2001; Zhang 2011).

There are a number of interesting connections or points of overlap between Deleuze and some of McLuhan's ideas. Significantly, Deleuze makes the point that any medium can be approached as a mode of expression, and that as a mode of expression it has 'different creative possibilities' (Deleuze 1995, 131). This is precisely the manner in which Guattari also conceptualises not just any medium, but technology in general. For example, in relation to computers, Guattari writes that '[i]t was a mistake on the part of structuralism to prioritise natural language which avoids technology' (Guattari 1995), pointing to the example of how 'computer-aided design leads to the production of images opening on to unprecedented plastic universes ... or to the solution of mathematical problems which would have been quite unimaginable a few years ago' (Guattari 1995, 5).

It is important to note that neither Deleuze, nor Guattari, nor McLuhan for that matter (Deleuze 1995, 131), adopt the view that technology determines our behaviour. Nor do either Deleuze or Guattari celebrate or necessarily hold any one medium as superior over another, even if they seem dismissive of television at times. While each different medium might hold different creative possibilities, or, perhaps rather, open up a different capacity for action or thought, what matters above all for them is that different media, those different modes of expression, are 'all related insofar as they must counter the introduction of a cultural space of markets and conformity – that is, a space of "producing for the market" – together' (Deleuze 1995, 131). Or, as Guattari phrases it, '[w]e should neither celebrate and critically nor reject totally these innovations – everything depends on [the] articulation within collective assemblages of enunciation' (Guattari 1995). This particular point concerning what Guattari calls 'assemblages of enunciation', especially with respect to the production of subjectivity, is critical. It is through exploring their approach to technology, and specifically their conceptualisation of the machine, that we find one manner in which to come to terms with their notion of the assemblage. In this way we can understand better the production of subjectivity and the function of media in that process.

Guattari offers us Franciso Varela's definition of the machine as one useful starting point here: a machine is 'the ensemble of the interrelations of its components, independent of the components themselves' (Varela in Guattari 1993, 16). If we adopt this approach to understanding what a machine is it should be immediately clear that a machine's materiality and a machine's organisation have little to do with one another. Stated differently, what constitutes any machine are less its actual material components, and more the manner in which those components are arranged in relation to each other. One example that helps to illustrate this is to consider the sorts of bureaucratic machines that Kafka described, in which people are constituted, and constitute themselves, as components of a larger (bureaucratic) machine (Deleuze and Guattari 1986), a machine that in some respects shares some of the components of the large-scale social machines that Mumford wrote of when he described the labour force that built the pyramids in Ancient Egypt:

> a machine of a hundred thousand manpower, that is, the equivalent, roughly, of ten thousand horsepower: a machine composed of a multitude of uniform, specialised, interchangeable, but functionally differentiated parts, rigorously marshalled together and coordinated in a process centrally organised and centrally directed: each part behaving as a mechanical component of the mechanised whole: unmoved by an internal impulse that would interfere with the working of the mechanism. (Mumford 1995, 318)

As Mumford further explains:

> To call these collective entities machines is no idle play on words. If a machine be defined more or less in accord with the classic definition of Reuleaux, as a combination of resistant parts, each specialised in function, operating under human control, to transmit motion and to perform work, then the labour machine was a real machine: all the more because its component parts, though composed of human bone, nerve, and muscle, were reduced to their bare mechanical elements and rigidly restricted to the performance of their mechanical tasks. (Mumford 1995, 315–16)

What is critical to recognise here is that machines are immediately and always social as well. As Deleuze and Guattari state:

[A] machine is never simply technical. Quite the contrary, it is technical only as a social machine, taking men and women into its gears, or, rather, having men and women as part of its gears along with things, structures, metals, materials. Even more, Kafka doesn't think only about the conditions of alienated, mechanized labor – he knows all about that in great, intimate detail – but his genius is that he considers men and women to be part of the machine not only in their work but even more so in their adjacent activities, in their leisure, in their loves, in their protestations, in their indignations, and so on. (Deleuze and Guattari 1986, 81)

This social aspect of the machine is critical throughout Deleuze and Guattari's work, and is a point that is always heavily emphasised in their *Anti-Oedipus*, where they repeatedly point out that what they term 'desiring-machines' don't 'exist outside the social machines that they form on a large scale; and no social machines without the desiring-machines that inhabit them on a small scale' (Deleuze and Guattari 1983, 340). Furthermore, desiring-machines 'and the multiplicities they constitute are inseparable from the social machines or social aggregates, and "constitute one and the same process of production"' (Savat and Thompson 2015, 284). When considered in this context the so-called technical machine, what we might consider 'technology' in the more traditional sense of the term, 'is only a piece in a social assemblage that it presupposes' (Deleuze and Guattari 1986, 82), or, as Deleuze and Guattari elsewhere write:

[T]he principle behind all technology is to demonstrate that a technical element remains abstract, entirely undetermined, as long as one does not relate it to an assemblage it presupposes. It is the machine that is primary in relation to the technical element: not the technical machine, itself a collection of elements, but the social or collective machine, the machinic assemblage that determines what is a technical element at a given moment, what is its usage, extension, comprehension, etc. (Deleuze and Guattari 1987, 397–8)

It is by way of this reasoning that Deleuze can argue that:

Types of machine are easily matched with each type of society
– not that machines are determining, but because they express

those social forms capable of generating them and using them. The old societies of sovereignty made use of simple machines – levers, pulleys, clocks; but the recent disciplinary societies equipped themselves with machines involving energy, with the passive danger of entropy and the active danger of sabotage; the societies of control operate with machines of a third type, computers, whose passive danger is jamming and whose active one is piracy and the introduction of viruses. (Deleuze 1992, 6)

This should also make clear why Deleuze and Guattari hold no simple technological determinist view: 'The very general primacy of the collective and machinic assemblage over the technical element applies generally, for tools as for weapons. Weapons and tools are consequences, nothing but consequences' (Deleuze and Guattari 1987, 398). This is a point that applies equally to the stirrup (1987, 399) as well as modes of expression or mediums: they are nothing but consequences, effects, whether they come in the form of statements, books, phones or televisions.

Of course, as the quotes from Deleuze and Guattari above make clear, particular sorts of consequences belong to particular sorts of societies. As Buchanan explains, '[g]iven a certain effect, what machine could have produced it?' (Buchanan 2008, 119). It is for this reason that Deleuze and Guattari make the important point that we should never consider technologies, tools or machines in isolation (Deleuze and Guattari 1987, 90). With this they mean that our tools, including our mediums, the things that make up the so-called materiality, the concreteness, of the (social) assemblages that we find ourselves situated in, as well as constituted as a component of, the so-called materiality of an assemblage, relate

[n]ot to the production of goods but rather to a precise state of intermingling of bodies in a society, including all the attractions and repulsions, sympathies and antipathies, alterations, amalgamations, penetrations, and expansion that affects bodies of all kinds in their relations to one another. (Deleuze and Guattari 1987, 90)

The stirrup, which is one example that Deleuze and Guattari use, 'entails a new man–horse symbiosis that at the same time entails new weapons and new instruments ... [Tools] presuppose a social machine that selects them and takes them into its "phylum": a society is defined by its amalgamations, not by its tools' (Deleuze and Guattari 1987, 90). In short, it is the connections between components, the organisation of those connections, the organisation of relations, the assemblage or arrangement (Buchanan 2015), that constitutes the machine. As Deleuze points out in *Cinema I*:

> If one had to define the whole, it would be defined by Relation. Relation is not a property of objects, it is always external to its terms. It is also inseparable from the open, and displays a spiritual or mental existence. Relations do not belong to objects, but to the whole, on condition that this is not confused with a closed set of objects.[1] (Deleuze 1986, 10)

For Deleuze this applies just as equally to tools as it does to images, language and words. Just as much as '[t]here is a primacy of the machinic assemblage of bodies over tools and goods, [there is] a primacy of the collective assemblage of enunciation over language and words' (Deleuze and Guattari 1987, 90) – that is, language and words similarly presuppose a social machine that selects and uses them.

If we further reconsider Varela's definition of the machine above, as well as Mumford's for that matter, we can immediately recognise how Deleuze and Guattari clearly think of assemblages as being machine-like, or 'machinic', as they term it. This is no metaphor for them. What constitutes any given assemblage or arrangement, or, rather, what enables us to recognise any specific assemblage from another, is the manner in which its components are organised in relation to each other. The assemblage is not made visible by the actual materiality of those components. In this way we can begin to recognise that some components might exist over a long period of time, and as such across various assemblages, but can be organised in quite different ways in relation to other components that form any other assemblage. Writing, as a technique or technology, for example, is a component that can operate in quite different ways depending on how it is organised in relation to other components. This is not to say that individual components cannot in some way transform an assemblage, or at least enable a transformation. Writing, as a communication technology, opened up the possibility of an entirely different way of acting in the world, including thinking about the world (Ong 2000). Writing also introduced a new human–book symbiosis that entailed new ways of acting in the world. A writer in that respect 'isn't a writer-man; he is a machine-man, and an experimental man' (Deleuze and Guattari 1987, 7). In this way we can recognise that habits, institutions, entire ways of living, have as a component 'writing as machine', which traverses so many of our assemblages, including the assemblage that is subjectivity. Writing, as a medium, as a technology, is so bound up in how we think about, organise and situate ourselves in the world. For example, sentences such as 'I'll look that up' would not be possible without writing (Ong 2000). These phrases are now simply habits. In that context consider how the mobile phone acts as a writing machine as well as a memory machine today. Prior to the mobile phone people would remember each other's phone numbers, but in the context of mobile phone use today most of us not only don't remember people's phone numbers, but we typically wouldn't even have looked at, or should we say 'looked up', the number in the first place. The digital assemblage has made that particular 'writing machine' redundant and thus changed the way we live.

It should be immediately clear then that any assemblage, especially the large-scale social assemblages noted so far, consists of a tremendous diversity of components. Deleuze and Guattari themselves offer us the following example to help illustrate the point:

> Taking the feudal assemblage as an example, we would have to consider the interminglings of bodies defining feudalism: the body of the earth and the social body; the body of the overlord, vassal, serf; the body of the knight and the horse and their new relation to the stirrup; the weapons and tools assuring a symbiosis of bodies – a whole machinic assemblage. We would also have to consider statements, expressions, the juridical regime of heraldry, all of the incorporeal transformations, in particular, oaths and their variables (the oath of obedience, but also the oath of love, etc.): the collective assemblage of enunciation. (Deleuze and Guattari 1987, 89)

This point too echoes that of Mumford:

> [o]ur mechanical civilisation represents the convergence of numerous habits, ideas, and modes of living, as well as technical instruments; and some of these were, in the beginning, directly opposed to the civilisation they helped to create. (Mumford 1995, 324)

Deleuze and Guattari are making it clear that an assemblage includes every part of the system, including the material, the social and the psychological aspects. However, assemblages do not only exist on such a large scale as historical epochs. Indeed, our subjectivity, or our sense of self or individuality, can itself be viewed as an assemblage, as something that we actively assemble and maintain, as well as something that we are assembled or arranged as. Guattari offers the following definition of subjectivity in this regard: 'the ensemble of conditions which render possible the emergence of individual and/or collective instances as self-referential existential Territories, adjacent, or in a delimiting relation, to an alterity that is itself subjective' (Guattari 1995, 9). So, subjectivity for Guattari is 'an ensemble of conditions', that is, it is an assemblage, a collective assemblage of enunciation, and as such 'does not correspond either to an individual entity or to a predetermined social entity' (Guattari and Rolnik 2008, 43). In this way we can immediately recognise that an assemblage or arrangement is something that is also processual, that it is in process, that is, flow. In this way Deleuze and Guattari propose that we think of subjectivity precisely as a process of production and individuation, whereby we produce and maintain a relative sense of unicity as *individuals*, and which we continuously (aim to) maintain in the face of a 'diversity of components of subjectivation' (Guattari 1995, 16), which flow through us and constitute us. Subjectivity, a collective assemblage of enunciation, indeed any assemblage, is an ongoing production, an ongoing arrangement of relations. This ongoing arrangement is what constitutes any assemblage.

The assemblages Deleuze and Guattari analyse range quite significantly in scale. As noted above, they think of large-scale social machines as assemblages, just as much as they might think of a person driving a car or reading a book as an assemblage, or, indeed, a person writing an e-mail or a text message as an assemblage. Equally importantly, they recognise that assemblages are machinic in character, that is, they constitute an ongoing process of production. Again, the key point here is that what constitutes any given assemblage is the actual connection between the components, rather than simply the components themselves:

> [T]he whole remains the same insofar as it is defined by a relation through which any of its parts belong to that particular modal essence. An existing mode is thus subject to considerable and continual alteration: but it little matters, either, that the division between its parts of movement and rest, or of speed and slowness of movement, should alter. A given mode will continue to exist as long as the same relation subsists in the infinite whole of its parts. (Deleuze 2005, 208)

In this respect they very much have a topological understanding of the assemblage:

> In topology two shapes are regarded as the same if you can bend, twist, stretch, or otherwise deform one into the other continuously – that is, without any ripping or puncturing. Unlike the rigid objects of geometry, the objects of topology behave as if they were infinitely elastic, as if they were made of an ideal kind of rubber or Silly Putty. (Strogatz 2012, 220)

This is precisely how Deleuze defines duration:

> [W]hile our body exists, it endures, and is defined by duration; its present state is inseparable from a previous state with which it is linked in continuous duration. Thus *to every idea that indicates an actual state of our body, there is necessarily linked another sort of idea that involves the relation of this state to the earlier state.* Spinoza explains that this should not be thought of as an abstract intellectual operation by which the mind compares two states. Our feelings are themselves ideas which involve the concrete relation of present and past in a continuous duration: they involve the changes of an existing mode that endures. (Deleuze 2005, 220 [emphasis original])

In looking at what constitutes any given assemblage, any given mode, Deleuze's focus is on the discontinuous spaces and formations that compose machines at certain points. I might be playing on a console one hour, and the next hour be reading a book, and the next be driving a car (Guattari and Rolnik 2008, 44). My body as a component connects to different components in enabling each of these activities. It is the process of connecting that (re)constitutes or repeats any given assemblage. More to the point, it is the ongoing and unceasing organisation (assembling or arranging) of the connections that is key to understanding the formation, the production, of assemblages. What organises that arrangement is what Deleuze and Guattari refer to as abstract machines, organising principles if you like, or what they sometimes elsewhere refer to as the Body without Organs (BwO). One example they offer of such an abstract machine is what they refer to as faciality, which they argue is a key machine in the production of subjectivity in capitalism, operating not simply in terms of how faces are constituted or organised, but how images in general function in the media and commodity culture.

While we explore the operation of faciality in how images function in society in the following chapter, the key point to emphasise is that playing on a games console, reading a book and driving a car are processual activities. Not only that, but as processual activities they not only form an assemblage in their own right, but they themselves function as parts of the formation of other assemblages. Indeed, in the process of connecting to other components those very activities can transform us as a component in the process. Even something as simple as an increase in speed, for example the difference between cycling to work and driving a car to work, changes our perception of the world and how we situate ourselves in that world. Or, if we want to consider a specific media device:

> Young people walking in the street with Walkmans establish a relation with music that is not 'natural.' In producing this kind of instrument (both as a means and as a content of communication), this highly sophisticated industry does not simply transmit specific music or organise natural sounds. What it is doing is inventing a musical universe, a different relation with musical objects: music that comes from within and not from somewhere outside. In other words, what it is doing is inventing a new perception. (Guattari and Rolnik 2008, 45)

In this respect, the body for Deleuze and Guattari can be understood as being constituted at any given moment of a variety of components and assemblages, or, more precisely, of a range of flows that traverse through us and which are cut, because an assemblage, being processual, is precisely composed as a flow and the cuts of a flow, a streamline of flows. As Deleuze states: '*to exist is to actually possess a very great number of parts.* These component parts are external to the mode's essence, and external one to another: they are extensive parts' (Deleuze 2005, 201) (emphasis original).

Critically, the resultant assemblies can have both a negative as well as a positive effect, in that some connections and resultant assemblages enhance a body's capacity for action, whereas others reduce that capacity. Here Deleuze's notion of affect is significant (Rizzo 2012, 66). As Shouse explains in relation to music:

> the pleasure [we] derive from music has less to do with the communication of meaning, and far more to do with the way that a particular piece of music 'moves' [us] [...] Every form of communication where facial expressions, respiration, tone of voice, and posture are perceptible can transmit affect, and that list includes nearly every form of mediated communication other than the one you are currently experiencing. (Shouse 2005)

We explore the importance of affect further in the following chapter in the context of image machines, but the key point is that affect is pre-personal, and is precisely a product, an activation, a connection between two different components. Affect, in short, is a particular flow between components or points. In this way a horse, a fish, a person – an assemblage or mode of existence – has a different capacity to be affected; each will not be affected by the same things or even in the same ways by the same things (Deleuze 2005, 217). In this respect, an assemblage 'ceases to exist when it can no longer maintain between its parts the relation that characterises it; and it ceases to exist when "it is rendered completely incapable of being affected in many ways." In short, relations are inseparable from the capacity to be affected' (Deleuze 2005, 218).

What concerns Deleuze is that the flows that are constituted are channelled, regulated or coded in particular sorts of ways. Indeed, the very function of society is to code flows, all kinds of flows: it is society's 'business' (Deleuze and Guattari 1983, 139). More specifically what concerns Deleuze is how capitalism as a social form of organisation, unlike previous societies, operates precisely by way of a process of uncoding or deterritorialisation: that is, it operates partly through a process of destruction, only to immediately recode flows for a different purpose. In part this purpose is the extraction of value, of money, a particular kind of flow. This is precisely why they are so concerned with those assemblages through which media operate, because much of what we refer to as media operate precisely to produce a particular form of culture, mass commodity culture, and produce us as subjects as part of this. Our flows, our desire, are unarranged and rearranged, unassembled and reassembled, uncoded and recoded, unorganised and reorganised, to produce that perhaps most mass-produced commodity of all in capitalism: subjectivity. Worryingly, for Deleuze and Guattari, we are quite willing participants in that production. In this way we desire our own repression. Media, as distribution machines, play a series of key functions in distributing and organising the flow of desire in this way, as we explore throughout this book. Some see digital media and the internet as helping us to avoid that machinic production of subjectivity, and both Deleuze and Guattari see some hope precisely in these interactive media (Harper 2009a). However, much of digital media, especially so-called social media, is involved in the production of a repressive subjectivity, and yet it is something that so many of us happily participate in. We desire, we assemble and arrange it.

In this respect, Deleuze's work is well placed to examine the production of the different, that is, avoiding a repetition of the same. However, as both Deleuze and Guattari stress throughout their work, they see increasingly little capacity in media, including digital media, for the new and 'outlandish' (deterritorialised) to emerge (Deleuze and Parnet 2012), or for new singularities to form that could escape the capturing and recoding by capitalism (Guattari and Rolnik 2008). Important in that regard is Deleuze's view that we are multiple, and not a unity (Smith 2012, 69). Desire is precisely not one, not individual. Desire, the flows of desire, 'the state of our unconscious drives and inclinations' (Smith 2012, 71), is precisely what is recoded, reterritorialised by capitalism, in the form of the One. We see such celebrations of the One everywhere in and by way of our media, from celebrity to Facebook. In short, it is in large part through the operation or production of what we call 'culture' that the production of subjectivity proceeds. It is in this way that our desire is recoded as interest, and in this way it is clear that this is not OUR interest.

Desire in this respect is productive, and not constituted, defined or to be understood in terms of lack, as in 'I desire that which I am not or do not have'. Desire is something that we *do* (Buchanan 2008, 48), and not some longing for that which we do not have. The machine, the assemblage, *is* desire: 'To enter or leave the machine, to be in the machine, to walk around it, to approach it – these are all still components of the machine itself: these are states of desire, free of all interpretation' (Deleuze and Guattari 1986, 7). Assemblages, the institutions that operate in our society, in our hearts and minds, are our desires, they are 'compositions of desire' and not 'a natural or spontaneous determination' (Deleuze and Guattari 1987, 399). Whether it be the policewoman giving a person a speeding fine, a man building a boat, a couple dancing, a manager trying to make his organisation more efficient, an administrator signing a form, an academic writing an e-mail, a boy reading a book, a girl playing on her console:

> in all these circumstances there is no desire but assembling, assembled, desire. The rationality, the efficiency, of an assemblage does not exist without the passions the assemblage brings into play, without the desires that constitute it as much as it constitutes them. (Deleuze and Guattari 1987, 399)

In this respect we cannot be against machines, against technology, against particular media per se. Our machines are us, and we are our machines. This is not to state that machines can't produce wholly negative modes of experience or existence, but, as Deleuze and Guattari continuously stressed, our machines, including our technical machines, are precisely us:

> There isn't a desire for power; it is power itself that is desire. Not a desire-lack, but desire as a plenitude, exercise, and functioning, even in the most subaltern of workers. Being an assemblage, desire is precisely one with the gears and the components of the machine, one with the power of the machine. And the desire that someone has for power is only his [*sic*] fascination for these gears, his [*sic*] desire to make certain of these gears going into

operation, to be himself [*sic*] one of these gears – or, for want of anything better, to be the material treated by these gears, a material that is a gear in its own way. (Deleuze and Guattari 1986, 55–6)

One such machine for Deleuze and Guattari is the book. In the first instance, a book might appear as an inanimate object, an object that passively just lies on a table. However, Deleuze and Guattari take the view that '[a] book is itself a little machine' (Deleuze and Guattari 1987, 4). A book, being a machine, must necessarily produce. Certainly, when we pick up a book, even when we haven't started reading yet, it already produces. In picking up a novel and looking at the title, thoughts are already produced in our head, for example. In this way it is already productive, constitutes a connection and flow, in the simplest of ways. At the same time, the book, being a machine, necessarily consists of components. That is, 'the book' is not so much the material object, but rather a specific organisation of components that we recognise as 'book'. These components are rather diverse, and may exist in some books, but not in other books, though perhaps what all books consist of is a strict separation of the writer and the reader (Ong 2000), unless we are dealing with digital interactive books, if we can still refer to these as 'books'. Of course, the printed book's universe of action is of a different order from the handwritten book. The printed book already heralds mass commodity culture, and more so than the handwritten book is associated with the notion of the private individual reading silently, alone (Eisenstein 1979; Ong 2000), though it is important to stress on this point that this is not a function of the materiality of the book as such, but a function of desire, that is, the social machine that is capable of producing that particular image of the book. It is in this way that the social machine, desire, establishes a principle of sameness in this particular image of the book – a notion of the common through the simple fact of requiring a more universal and uniform language, and distributing that sameness, that commonality. It is in this way that the book is so strongly associated with the state, as well as science, in its codification of flow – capitalism couldn't function without the figure of the book and its centrality in the development of accounting, mapping the flows and extracting from them a value (Eisenstein 1979; Smith 2011). We already see so many assemblages that constitute themselves in and by way of the book.

There is, of course, also the notion of 'the author', the individual that we today so strongly associate with the book and who we celebrate, which was not always a component of the book. Indeed, the figure of the author is a relatively recent phenomenon, developing precisely in tangent with particular notions of ownership that are central to capitalism (Poster 2001). This notion of authorship Deleuze and Guattari immediately examine in their opening to *A Thousand Plateaus*, where they remind us that they are not two authors, but several authors, and as such a crowd. The reason they still have their name on the book, they explain, is because it is in large part to 'render imperceptible, not ourselves, but what makes us act, feel, and think' (Deleuze and Guattari 1987, 3). It might also have to do with the publishers and the need to code flows. But they also do it because it is a habit, 'because it's nice to talk like everybody else, to say the sun rises, when everybody knows it's only a manner of speaking' (1987, 3). We already noted Ong's point regarding the habitual aspect of the phrase 'look something up' – these ideas become a habit. The notion of authorship, in short, Deleuze and Guattari claim, is also a habit, an assemblage that repeats itself, and is something they also challenge throughout their work. The more important question in that respect is: What is the machine that is capable of producing the effect of authorship, and how does that machine work? How can that machine be made to function, produce, differently?

This is exactly part of what *A Thousand Plateaus* aims to do. The opening paragraph of 'Introduction: Rhizome' raises precisely a question concerning the effect of authorship. There is already a question as to who the thought in the book can be or should be attributed to. Who is it exactly that speaks to us? Or more precisely, since we just used a manner of speaking out of pure habit as well – nobody 'speaks' in a book – as we do so often, who is it exactly that writes to us, and why do we even ask that question? Why is it important that we know who speaks? Immediately, we already begin to challenge a key aspect of what we think about when we think about books, and, indeed, a key aspect of what we think about when we think about thought.

A book, Deleuze and Guattari write,

has neither object nor subject; it is made of variously formed matters, and very different dates and speeds. To attribute the book to a subject is to overlook this working of matters, and the exteriority of their relations. It is to fabricate a beneficent God to explain geological movements. In a book, as in all things, there are lines of articulation or segmentarity, strata and territories; but also lines of flight, movements of deterritoriali- sation and destratification. Comparative rates of flow on these lines produce phenomena of relative slowness and viscosity, or, on the contrary, of acceleration and rupture. All this, lines and measurable speeds, constitutes an *assemblage*. (Deleuze and Guattari 1987, 3–4)

A book, then, is an assemblage, a multiplicity, and for this reason cannot be attributed to a specific subject. Furthermore, they claim it has no object either, when they state that '[t]here is no difference between what a book talks about and how it is made' (1987, (4), and that a book 'has only itself in connection with other assem- blages ...' For this reason they will never ask what a book means nor 'look for anything to understand in it'. Instead, they 'will ask what it functions with, in connection with what other things it does or does not transmit intensities, in which other multiplicities its own are inserted and metamorphosed', stating that '[a] book exists only through the outside and on the outside' (Deleuze and Guattari 1987, 4). As in their other work, they are not interested in asking what something means, but are principally interested in how something functions. In short, in order to establish how a book forms an assemblage, we need to ask how does a book function, and, as part of that question, in relation to what does it function? In other words, what does a book connect with, how does it connect and what does it produce?

It is in this context that Deleuze and Guattari identify three types of book-machines, or, to be more precise, three models or images of thought. The first type of book they identify is what they call the 'root-book':

This is the classical book, as noble, signifying, and subjective organic interiority (the strata of the book). The book imitates the world, as art imitates nature: by procedures specific to it that accomplish what nature cannot or can no longer do. The law of the book is the law of reflection, the One that becomes two. How could the law of the book reside in nature, when it is what presides over the very division between world and book, nature and art? One becomes two: whenever we encounter this formula, even stated strategically by Mao or understood in the most 'dialectical' way possible, what we have before us is the most classical and well-reflected, oldest, and weariest kind of thought. Nature doesn't work that way [...] (Deleuze and Guattari 1987, 5)

Here they invoke the image of the tree, arborescence, as the image of thought. 'Even the book as a natural reality is a taproot, with its pivotal spine and surrounding leaves' (Deleuze and Guattari 1987, 5). This is an image of thought in which thought proceeds neatly in a binary fashion, much like the branches of a tree, or a pivotal taproot. In this way one always becomes two, endlessly proliferating in a binary fashion: x or y. A so-called rational, logical, model of thought. This is a system, a model, of thought that dominates so much of our thinking, and entirely incapable of understanding multiplicity, assemblages. This is a model of thought that begins with the One, the original – it has a beginning – and every other thought is a copy, an imitation, something that stands for the 'real thing', as well as a proliferation – always at least one move from the original, in pursuit of some lack, some guilt to alleviate, an endless proliferation of representations.

A second book-machine or type of book that Deleuze and Guattari identify is the 'radicle-system, or fascicular root [...] to which our modernity pays willing allegiance' (Deleuze and Guattari 1987, 5). This model of thought we find in the work of people such as William Burroughs, but also Joyce and Nietzsche. In such books, in such models of thought, the world becomes chaos (Deleuze and Guattari 1987, 6). Here 'the world has lost its pivot; the subject can no longer even dichotomise, but accedes to a higher unity, of ambivalence and overdetermination, in an always supplementary dimension to that of its object' (Deleuze and Guattari 1987, 6). Yes, we have multiplicity here, a recognition of multiplicity, but always a multiplicity that ultimately is reduced to a totality – the proliferation of thought here always moves in a linear direction, while 'a unity of totalisation asserts itself even more firmly in another, circular or cyclic, dimension' (Deleuze and Guattari 1987, 6). In short, this is a system that does not break with dualism, and which maintains a complementarity between subject and object, 'a natural reality and a spiritual reality' (Deleuze and Guattari 1987, 6). In other words, this type of book, this image of thought, continues to function as a model of representation, even if it has more capacity to recognise the operation of multiplicity. It remains an arborescent model of thought. We all have trees growing in our heads, as they state, but also that they are 'tired of trees. We should stop believing in trees, roots, and radicles. They've made us suffer too much. All of arborescent culture is founded on them, from biology to linguistics' (Deleuze and Guattari 1987, 15). The tree and root, as they state, 'inspire a sad image of thought that is forever imitating the multiple on the basis of a centred or segmented higher unity' (Deleuze and Guattari 1987, 16).

The key issue for Deleuze, which he pursues in a variety of ways throughout his work, is that thought is precisely not binary, not a representation, not an imitation and not the thought of the One. Thought is not neat, 'logical', 'rational', and does not involve a subject that reflects on an object. Instead, Deleuze and Guattari propose that 'the brain itself is much more a grass than a tree' (Deleuze and Guattari 1987, 15). Thought is not tree-like, arborescent, but takes the form of a rhizome, is a rhizome. Indeed, not just thought:

> [T]he question is whether plant life in its specificity is not entirely rhizomatic. Even some animals are, in their pack form. Rats are rhizomes. Burrows are too, in all of their functions of shelter, supply, movement, evasion, and breakout. The rhizome itself assumes very diverse forms, from ramified surface extension in all directions, to concretion into bulbs and tubers. When rats swarm over each other. The rhizome includes the best and the worst: potato and couchgrass, or the weed. Animal and plant, couchgrass is crabgrass. (Deleuze and Guattari 1987, 6–7)

This is a model of thought in which there is no beginning or end. Deleuze and Guattari emphasise that thought is precisely 'always in the middle, between things, interbeing, *intermezzo*' (Deleuze and Guattari 1987, 25). Thought is precisely flow. A flow, a fluid, is a substance that flows, and as such is not defined by movement. Fluids, flows, do not move, they flow. They have a rate of flow, they have speed, but flows do not move from A to B. As Deleuze and Guattari state:

the middle is by no means an average; on the contrary, it is where things pick up speed. Between things does not designate a localisable relation going from one thing to the other and back again, but a perpendicular direction, a transversal movement that sweeps one *and* the other away, a stream without beginning or end that undermines its banks and picks up speed in the middle. (Deleuze and Guattari 1987, 25)

The image of thought they associate with the tree, with arborescence, 'imposes the verb "to be"'. The tree is about filiation, as in the way we see this explored in shows such as *Who Do You Think You Are?* They always trace a filiation, draw a tree. The rhizome does not concern itself with filiation, but with alliances: 'the fabric of the rhizome is the conjunction, "and ... and ... and ..."' Questions such as 'Who do you think you are?', 'Where do you come from?', 'Where are you going?', 'these are totally useless questions [...] all imply a false conception of voyage and movement' (Deleuze and Guattari 1987, 25). The rhizome, thought, desire, is precisely not complete, always n−1, 'the only way the one belongs to the multiple: always subtract' (Deleuze and Guattari 1987, 6), always in process, always flowing. It is in this way that they state that the multiple cannot be found, but must be made. This is precisely creativity. This is precisely desire, that is, assemblage, arranging flows.

As Smith (2012) explains, Deleuze inverts Plato's representational model of thought. Deleuze inverts the model of thought that dominates so much of thought and of our thinking, especially about media. This representational model of thought is a model where signs are always somehow one step removed from the real, always somehow defined by what they are not, always defined by what they can only ever resemble in varying degrees – always a copy, an imitation in some way, not the 'real' thing. In such a model of thought the very idea of difference is always defined by what it is not, always a lack, always guilty somehow, always defined negatively, and never defined positively, never defined in its own positive power. Deleuze's move is 'to show' – here 'our' language perhaps betrays us – that signs have their own productive power. Signs, thoughts, desire, assemblages, that is, simulacra for Deleuze (Smith 2012, 26), operate without resemblance to some real. Instead, assemblages, as we explore in the following chapter, and what are termed their abstract machines, their organising principles, are the structure of the virtual (Deleuze and Guattari 1994, 209). These structures are what organise the real, that is, actualise the real (Smith 2012, 26). This is the reason why Deleuze provokes us to ask not what something means, not ask where something comes from, not ask questions such as 'what is', which belong to arborescent thought and are questions of resemblance. Instead, he, together with Guattari, asks that we become mechanics, and ask how something works, what its role is in the process of production. What machine, what assemblage, produces those particular effects and how does it do that? They especially provoke us to think about the effect, the product that is subjectivity. This is a product that in our society is so deeply tied to the notion of the One, the individual, the origin, personified precisely in the figure of the author and the celebration of such individuality: the pop star, the movie star – we all need our fifteen minutes of fame. No wonder we desired social media. Facebook came just in time: let me show you my face, let me show you desire.

CHAPTER TWO

Image machines

There is at some moment a calm and restful world.
Suddenly a frightened face looms up [...]

(DELEUZE AND GUATTARI 1994, 17)

The face is the vampire [...]

(DELEUZE 1986, 99)

The very first time I saw your face I thought of a song and
quickly changed the tune.

(SMITH, TOLHURST AND GALLUP 1981)

Images proliferate all around us in everyday life. Whether we are watching television, looking at a painting, surfing the World Wide Web, watching a YouTube clip, reading a newspaper or magazine or watching a movie, we increasingly live in an image world (Morse 1998). Even writing and print are in the first instance visual media, and it is useful in this context to keep in mind that different writing systems from around the world developed from drawings and images. Of course, many of us experience images increasingly through the interface and frame of the screen, whether these be television screens, touch screens or projections of images on a wall or the retina. Indeed, many people carry their screens with them in the form of the smartphone, and often communicate with each other sometimes solely through images, whether this be in the form of emoticons or emojis, or in the form of photographs posted on social media, as is the case with Instagram or Tumblr, for example.

There are different ways in which we can understand these images. In the first instance, we could approach images in terms of any representational function they may have. In such a view we ask referential questions about an image: 'What is this an image of? Is it realistic? Is it true?' (Morse 1998, 11). Of course, as will be clear from the previous chapters, these are precisely the sorts of questions that Deleuze suggests we avoid asking in the first instance. Instead, if we use Deleuze's approach, we should ask what it is that images *do*, or, more precisely, it is not that we should not ask about the meaning of an image, but we should do this in terms of its functional and not its semiotic sense (Buchanan 2008, 94). In other words, as part of what assemblage does an image function and what is its function in the constitution of that particular assemblage – what connections are established and maintained and what is produced, or capable of being produced, in the process of that connection?

It is immediately obvious that images certainly *do* something when we watch them. The moment we see an image, the moment we establish a connection with an image, something clearly happens. When we see the image of a dead Syrian child being carried by a state official on a beach in Greece – in particular the manner in which for many people the child's shoes evoke a particular response – what we feel galvanises particular social and political reactions; when the gaze of the camera is held in close-up on the face of a woman who has lost a loved one in a bomb attack, until the point that tears begin to roll down her face; when we watch the beheading of a journalist, even when we don't see the beheading itself; when we view the photographs or videos of the aftermath of Hurricane Katrina or the tsunami in Fukujima; when we see an image of George Clooney, and in particular the smile, being used in the advertising of a brand of coffee, wrist watches or whiskey; when we watch yet another funny cat video on YouTube; a romantic drama and the image of a couple kissing; when we see the photographs of a person's moments in life at his or her funeral, even if the person is a stranger to us: in all these situations it is immediately clear that something happens when we connect with images. That process of connection is clearly productive of something. As Deleuze explains of the image:

An image is, in the strictest sense, an imprint, a trace or physical impression, an affection of the body itself, the effect of some body on the soft and fluid parts of our own body; in the figurative sense, an image is the idea of an affection which makes an object known to us only by its effect. But such knowledge is not knowledge at all, it is at best recognition. (Deleuze 2005, 147)

In the first instance, when we think about the process of watching an image, we might be tempted to state that we are feeling something, that we are experiencing a particular emotion or set of emotions. It might be sadness, it might be anger, it might be laughter, tears of joy, exhilaration, despair, fear, doubt, contentment, resentment. However, from Deleuze's perspective, as the above quote of his suggests, this can be more usefully understood in terms of affect rather than emotion or feeling per se. As Brian Massumi explains in his notes on the translation of *A Thousand Plateaus* in relation to the terms affect and affection:

Neither word denotes a personal feeling. [Affect] is an ability to affect and be affected. It is a prepersonal intensity corresponding to the passage from one experiential state of the body to another and implying an augmentation or diminution in that body's capacity to act. (Massumi in Deleuze and Guattari 1987, xvi)

In that respect, affects are somewhat different from feelings, as the latter 'are personal and biographical' and involve the recognition of something previously experienced (Shouse 2005). Affects are also different from emotions as these are social, that is, 'the projection/display of a feeling. Unlike feelings, the display of emotion can be either genuine or feigned' (Shouse 2005). Affect is what pre-exists feeling and emotions, and exists independently of them, it 'is the change, or variation, that occurs when bodies collide, or come into contact' (Colman 2005, 11). Affect, then, is transformative; it 'acts on the body to transform it. It acts on the body's capacities' (Angel and Gibbs 2006, 35), and that transformation can either, in Spinoza's sense, be joyful or sad (Deleuze 2005), or, in Nietzsche's sense, active or reactive (Deleuze 2006), and it 'can be utilised to enable ability, authority, control and creativity' (Colman 2005, 12). As Deleuze and Guattari explain elsewhere, 'affects are becomings' (1987, 256).

It is also critical to recognise that affection is processual. After all, at work here is desire and the coding of desire. As Shouse explains, affection is

> the process whereby affect is transmitted between bodies. 'The transmission of affect means that we are not self-contained in terms of our energies. There is no secure distinction between the 'individual' and the 'environment' [...] The importance of affect rests upon the fact that in many cases the message consciously received may be of less import to the receiver of that message than his or her non-conscious affective resonance with the source of the message. (Shouse 2005)

One of several concepts through which Deleuze explains the operation of affect is that of faciality, and the latter is a particularly useful concept to come to terms with the function and operation of images, moving and still, as well as their operation in culture and society more generally. As Angel and Gibbs (2006) point out, when we look at the images that form our image world, faces – including emoticons and emojis – are literally everywhere. The face, they state, 'mediates most forms of visual communication' (Angel and Gibbs 2006, 25). Indeed, for Deleuze it is clear that the face plays an important role in communication in general, and not only on our screens. As Deleuze explains, in the face we can ordinarily identify three functions:

> it is individuating (it distinguishes or characterises each person); it is socialising (it manifests a social role); it is relational or communicating (it ensures not only communication between two people, but also, in a single person, the internal agreement between his character and his role). (Deleuze 1986, 101)

However, such an understanding of the face still leaves the face in the role of basically communicating some meaning, or as representing or communicating some evidence of what lies underneath the face, that is, it operates with an idea that there is something behind the appearance of a face. As Rushton (2002, 224) points out, this is very much a representational and Platonic approach to understanding the face; however, and as Deleuze and Guattari state, '[t]he face is not an envelope exterior to the person who speaks, thinks, or feels' (Deleuze and Guattari 1987, 167). Instead, to reach a different understanding of the function of the face Deleuze separates 'the expression of the face from the one who expresses' (Rushton 2002, 224). We then see the face 'in-itself' rather than a face that stands for something else so that, for example: 'instead of reading a perplexed face as that which stands for someone's perplexity, we encounter a pure quality or affect' of perplexity (Rushton 2002, 224). The face in that regard 'is not the material representative of immaterial motivations; the face is not the external effect of an interior cause,' but 'incorporates as part of itself the very feeling or idea' (Rushton 2002, 224–5).

Deleuze examines this operation or function of the face in *Cinema 1* (1986) by way of the close-up and the function of framing images more generally. For Deleuze, the face itself already is a close-up, rather than there being a 'close-up *of* the face' as such (Deleuze 1986, 88). On the first level, what the close-up in film does is enable the face to function separately from the body, that is, it enables the face to function as an autonomous entity, and in doing so destroys the ordinary triple function of the face as noted above by Deleuze (Smith 2012, 205). It is through the close-up that the face in itself, the face as autonomous entity, now functions as

> the building material of the affect, its 'hyle'. Hence these strange cinematographic nuptials in which the actress provides her face and the material capacity of her parts, whilst the director invents the affect or the form of the expressible which borrows and puts them to work. (Deleuze 1986, 103)

In the close-up, the face's capacity to communicate information, to distinguish one individual from another, as well as its socialising capacity, dissolves, is decontextualised (Herzog 2008, 68). In this way the close-up, through the act of framing, in the first instance deterritorialises the face (Flaxman and Oxman 2008) and opens up a new potential for the face that goes beyond its ordinary individuating, socialising or communicative functions. The face becomes an expression of the possible and 'the surface on which determinations will be mapped' (Flaxman and Oxman 2008, 44). Significantly, the act of framing in film does not simply deterritorialise the face, or rather, re-constitute the face as an autonomous entity, but rather 'the close-up is by itself face' (Deleuze 1986, 88). For Deleuze any image can function as face, as a particular type of surface. It could be the image of a clock, a close-up of a knife, a body-part, a cup. '*The affection-image is the close-up, and the close-up is the face* [...] It is both a type of image and a component in all images' (Deleuze 1986, 87) (emphasis original). As Deleuze and Guattari state elsewhere: 'The close-up in films pertains as much to a knife, cup, clock, or kettle as to a face or facial element [...] Is it not fair to say, then, that there are close-ups in Novels [...] and in painting [...]?' (1987, 175).

According to Deleuze and Guattari, the face can be found in operation everywhere, including images in general:

> the maternal power operating through the face during nursing; the passional power operating through the face of a loved one, even in caresses; the political power operating through the face of the leader (streamers, icons, and photographs), even in mass actions; the power of film operating through the face of the star and the close-up; the power of television. (Deleuze and Guattari 1987, 175)

Indeed, for Guattari '[F]aciality has become a substance that is found both everywhere and nowhere; it even constitutes the substance of semiological fields' (Guattari 2011a, 95). The face, according to Deleuze and Guattari, plays a central role in organising our world. More precisely, as Rushton explains, 'the face carries out a preorganization of the world upon which experiences are made possible: the face is virtual, while the experiences are actual' (Rushton 2002, 225–6). This virtual, the face, precedes the actual and it is precisely what enables particular forms of experience to be actualised. More to the point, the virtual organises, or, more precisely, *assembles* the actual. As Deleuze explains in *Difference and Repetition*, and this is an important point to stress, '[t]he reality of the virtual is structure' (1994, 209). In this way, for Deleuze, the virtual is just as real as the actual. It is in this manner that the face, as Deleuze and Guattari (1987) explain, functions as a 'substance of expression'. It is also important to note that it is not so much that art, for example, actualises virtual affects, 'rather, it gives them a "body, a life, a universe"' (Smith 2012, 205).

Again, what is at work here is a different model of communication than what is traditionally considered when we look at images. Rather than being based on models that operate with notions of sender–message–receiver, or signifier/signified, which rely on a distinction between original and copy and a notion of representation, the face for Deleuze pre-exists communication and is what makes communication possible (Rushton 2002, 225). The face, a particular surface, opens a particular universe of action. More precisely, the face is an assemblage, an ongoing process of assembly, a machine, one which Deleuze and Guattari term the abstract machine of faciality, and it is this abstract machine around which we organise our faces, though these are never our own: 'Faces are not basically individual; they define zones of frequency or probability, delimit a field that neutralises in advance any expressions or connections unamenable to the appropriate signi-fications' (Deleuze and Guattari 1987, 168). A simple example of how faces are not individual can perhaps be found in celebrities and the phenomenon of the movie star, including the manner in which they cultivate and replicate a particular 'look' across genera-tions, and which we see replicated in countless selfies posted on social media.

The face, or rather the abstract machine of faciality, sets the scene so to speak. This abstract machine is what enables the face to function in the ways that it does. As Deleuze and Guattari explain:

> Concrete faces cannot be assumed to come ready-made. They are engendered by an *abstract machine of faciality*, which produces them at the same time as it gives the signifier its white wall and subjectivity its black hole. Thus the black hole/white wall system is, to begin with, not a face but the abstract machine that produces faces according to changeable combinations of its cogwheels. Do not expect the abstract machine to resemble what it produces, or will produce. (Deleuze and Guattari 1987, 168)

This white wall and black hole form a system through the abstract machine of faciality operates. According to Deleuze and Guattari, faciality functions through two axes, one of which constitutes a reflective, unified surface (the while wall), and the other consti-tuting a multiplicity of parts (the black holes), and these two axes are intertwined and constantly shift (Herzog 2008, 68). Deleuze offers the example of the clock. On the one hand you can look at the clock as a whole, the face of the clock, which constitutes the reflective white wall, and on the other hand you can also look at the movement of the hands of the clock, which is an incremental and serial movement. Obviously, both exist simultaneously, but the key thing is that they constitute 'two "conditions of possibility" that can either open through serial movements to connect with other worlds or occupy the reflective space of the interval' (Herzog 2008, 69). It is this particular white wall/black hole system, also understood as the two axes of significance and subjectification, that establishes the operation of the face, and, more specifically, the idea of the face. While for Deleuze the close-up in cinema best demonstrates its operation, it doesn't even have to be close-ups that 'extract' faciality: 'shots that are not technically "close" can achieve the status of the close-up through the collapsing of depth, or the "suppression of perspective", such that the image elicits an affective power or quality' (Herzog 2008, 68).

The reason why Deleuze, as well as Guattari in his own work, focuses on the face in particular is because the face is so central to Western culture, and increasingly so if the way social media are organised is any measure. Facebook, a book of faces, which places each individual as central to its network of 'friends', is emblematic of this, as is the phenomenon of the selfie. As boyd and Ellison (2007) point out, ego-centrism is a key feature of how much of social media is organised. For Deleuze, as well as Guattari, under the conditions of capitalism faciality is centrally involved in the production of a particular form of subjectivity: the individual. Faciality as a machine assembles or constitutes faciality not only as a site of possible encounters that may produce something new, but, more worryingly for Deleuze 'it is an organising, and a limiting machine of capture' (Thompson and Cook 2013, 381):

> [F]aciality is an abstract machine that captures the multidimensional and polyvocal flows of possibility and forces them into one dimensionality and univocity. This is why the face is an ordering machine. The face is 'not content to cover the head, but touches all other parts of the body, and even, if necessary, other objects without resemblance'. (Thompson and Cook 2013, 381)

It is for precisely this reason that Deleuze and Guattari state that 'the face is a politics' (1987, 181). Deleuze and Guattari associate the abstract machine of faciality, the particular idea and organisation of the face so familiar to us, with only specific regimes of power, and it finds its most developed form in capitalist society. It is for this reason that Deleuze and Guattari explain that the face, the idea of the face, is not universal. Indeed, Deleuze and Guattari identify as one key point in the formation of the idea of the face the year zero in Western culture. 'The face is Christ' as they state (1987, 176). The reverence of Christ as the saviour through individual sacrifice, the continual representation of his individuality as somehow divine, sets in place a politics of isolated, guilty, individuality that would manifest itself for thousands of years as 'the perfect face'. It is in this context that they explain in a more concrete way the manner in which the face operates as an ordering and a capturing machine, central to which is 'the function of biunivocalisation, or binarisation' (1987, 176).

The abstract machine of faciality, that is, the machine that organises the face, is 'composed by a black hole/white wall system, [and] functions in two ways' (Deleuze and Guattari 1987, 176–7). The first function is that the black hole 'acts as a central computer, Christ, the third eye that moves across the wall or the white screen serving as a general frame of reference' (1987, 177). In the first instance, then, the machine already 'constitutes a facial unit, an elementary face in biunivocal relation with another' (1987, 177). This point about the relation is important, because it immediately sets a face up in relation to another face, what Deleuze and Guattari refer to as a four-eyed machine 'made of elementary faces linked two by two' (1987, 177). As they explain, the face 'is a man *or* a woman, a rich person or a poor one, an adult or a child, a leader or a subject "an x *or* a y"' (1987, 177) (emphasis original). It is on the basis of such units (x or y) that the abstract machine of faciality produces and transforms 'concrete individualised faces' (1987, 177).

The second function of this machine is that it also involves a choice:

[G]iven a concrete face, the machine judges whether it passes or not, whether it goes or not, on the basis of the elementary facial units. This time, the binary relation is of the 'yes–no' type. The empty eye or black hole absorbs or rejects, like a half-doddering despot who can still give a signal of acquiescence or refusal. The face of a given teacher is contorted by tics and bathed in anxiety that makes it 'no go'. A defendant, a subject, displays an overaffected submission that turns into insolence. Or someone is too polite to be honest. [...] At every moment, the machine rejects faces that do not conform, or seem suspicious. (Deleuze and Guattari 1987, 177)

Importantly, this is not typically a single moment of choice. The faciality machine continuously expands the white wall, the frame of reference, and the black hole continuously and repeatedly functions. In other words, the machine continuously expands and proliferates by establishing biunivocal relationships – x *or* y – and binary relations – yes *or* no. Man/woman, fat/slim, white/non-white, tall/short, rich/poor, beautiful/ugly, smart/stupid and so on, until a point is reached where the face no longer conforms: 'A ha! It's not a man and it's not a woman, so it must be a transvestite' (Deleuze and Guattari 1987, 177). It is this process, this gridding of the face through a set of categories, this mapping, whereby a tolerance is established or, indeed, an enemy. In short, the faciality machine– and it is important to stress any image can function in this way, not simply faces – is a 'deviance detector': it computes normalities (Deleuze and Guattari 1987, 177–8).

What is significant about the abstract machine of faciality is that its overall function is to produce normality: 'You will be pinned to the white wall and stuffed in the black hole' (Deleuze and Guattari 1987, 181). In that respect, faciality, in the example of racism, does not so much operate to establish an inside and an outside, does not so much operate through exclusion, but through 'the determination of degrees of deviance in relation to the White-Man face, which endeavours to integrate nonconforming traits into increasingly eccentric and backward waves' (1987, 178). As Elliot (2012, 85) points out, many in the media rely on a simple binary of insider or outsider, including politicians who elicit fear (Angel and Gibbs 2006) through terms such as citizen or refugee, refugee or illegal immigrant, included or excluded. Instead Deleuze and Guattari argue that racism 'is based not on otherness but "waves of sameness", not on the simple binary but on a spectrum of difference that recognises not exteriority, [but] only faces who differ from the white one' (Elliot 2012, 85). As Deleuze and Guattari explain, 'Racism never detects the particles of the other; it propagates waves of sameness until those who resist identification have been wiped out' (Deleuze and Guattari 1987, 178). The face, the idea of the face of Christ, according to Deleuze and Guattari, is the blueprint. Faciality, the black hole/white wall system that can function by way of any image, operates to produce a singular substance 'that must allow and ensure the almightiness of the signifier as well as the autonomy of the subject' (Deleuze and Guattari 1987, 181). The abstract machine of faciality, the idea of the face, the production of subjectivity in the form of 'the individual', establishes the frame of reference in the form of its ever expanding white wall and ever proliferating black holes. As Guattari explains it:

> There is signification: that's what's essential! And this facialised signification cannot allow any matter of expression to escape that would allow it to leak [...] Within the framework of capitalistic assemblages, such an escape hardly has any chance to happen – except in the rare moments of childhood, passion, madness, and creation. The individuation of the enunciation – as the relay of permanent social control over the production of statements – is literally obsessed with the threat of semiotic collapse. (Guattari 2011a, 78)

The function of the frame in that respect, especially when we look at the images that proliferate all around us in the media sphere, is especially significant. As Deleuze points out in *Cinema I*:

> framing is limitation. But, depending on the concepts itself the limits can be conceived in two ways, mathematically or dynamically: either as preliminary to the existence of the bodies whose essence they fix, or going as far as the power of existing bodies goes. (Deleuze 1986, 13)

The act of framing a shot is in the first instance a deterritorialisation. A close-up of a face suspends individuation in the first instance and liberates affect from the individual (Flaxman and Oxman 2008, 50). It is in the first instance a (de)selection, and separates 'the image from its larger milieu' (Flaxman and Oxman 2008, 45). As noted above, it is in this way that the face functions as a substance of expression, and enables the encounter of the new, establishes a zone of possibility.

However, what is equally critical about facialisation is that it is precisely engaged in the social production of face (Deleuze and Guattari 1987, 181). As Elliott (2012, 77) explains, the face 'is the point at which our inner intractable selves meet the social world of others and, in this, it is a powerful concept indeed'. This particular machine

> performs the facialization of the entire body and all its surroundings and objects, and the landscapification of all worlds and milieus. The deterritorialization of the body implies a reterritorialization on the face; the collapse of corporeal coordinates or milieus implies the constitution of a landscape. (Deleuze and Guattari 1987, 181)

This facialisation of the world, in short, is not only related to a particular abstract machine, but is also, and this is the equally critical point, related to 'particular assemblages of power that require that social production' (Deleuze and Guattari 1987, 181). For Deleuze and Guattari (1987, 182) capitalism is where the production of subjectivity in the form of individuality reaches its zenith. Capitalism precisely celebrates the individual, and operates through the production and valorisation of the individual, even while the individual is perhaps the most mass-produced and standardised commodity of capitalism. It is only in a society and culture 'that privileges the one over the many' that the face can have such a significant role (Elliot 2012, 83).

In recognising that the face functions as a mode of expression, enabling both the encounter of the new in its initial deterritorialisation of the body and milieu, as well as a capturing machine that reterritorialises and recodes the face, it should also be immediately clear that our faces are not our own. As Deleuze (2005, 146) explains, '[w]hat we call an "object" is only the effect an object has on our own body; what we call "me" is only the idea we have of our own body and our soul insofar as they suffer an effect'. Or, 'as the song says, "*I'm changing my shape, I feel like an accident*"' (Deleuze 2003, 127 [emphasis original]). Faces, in short, are not chosen:

> [A] concrete face is an actualisation of the virtual terrain – the gridding of subjectivity and subjectification. These axes of subjectification and significance are both spontaneous events

and copies or returns of previous faces. The face is both a unique event and a copy – a returning visage that resonates with the past but is not of the past. (Thompson and Cook 2013, 382)

Or, as Guattari explains:

The world and its faciality never cease intertwining their relations. A face is always tied to a landscape as its foundation in such a way that it shuts off in itself, shrivels away in the grips of an apparatus of power, or reopens on a line of flight in order to provide an exit toward other possibles. During the course of the day, I travel from one faciality to another. My typical expression at present is no more 'my own' than any other. It is perhaps even that of another; not necessarily that of another *person*. But also that of an animal, a plant, a constellation of objects, a familiar space, an institution – for example, the 'a priori' faciality of the doctor, the robotic face of the 'insane' or the police, or a landscape-faciality, or a professional, ethnic faciality, etc. (Guattari 2011a, 80–1)

The machine of faciality is in operation throughout society. We carry this machine in our heads and hearts – we are this machine. Whenever we look at a face, the machine is in operation – it deterritorialises and reterritorialises. When we are in the classroom, meet with our general practitioner, speak with our father, watch an advertisement for make-up or the latest car, or even see images of some tourist destination – in all these instances there is the constitution and production of face. Importantly, this is of course processual, as the above quote from Guattari makes clear. Faces are fluid (Thompson and Cook 2013). We have to work at producing and maintaining face. Indeed, we carry multiple faces, activate multiple faces in some situations: for example, the teacher in a classroom has to deal with many faces (Thompson and Cook 2013). The face in that respect should certainly not solely be understood as a surface, but also as immediately a relation, and a dynamic processual relation, not a static one, including when we view an image. It is in this respect as much a surface as a performance, a mask, though not a mask as we might more traditionally understand, as some surface that hides. Instead, the mask now is the face; it assures the 'abstraction and operation of the face. The inhumanity of the face' (Deleuze and Guattari 1987, 181). The uniform, for example, is 'a facialisation of the body, with buttons for black holes against the white wall of the material' (1987, 181).

When we focus more specifically on the image world around us, and the manner in which images operate as part of capitalism's more general regime of signs, we see the white wall/black holes' key function in producing that single substance of face. The media are critical in this process of subjectivation. As Angel and Gibbs (2006, 25) make clear, '[t]he face is one of the human attributes used by the media to cathect the human into flows of information and capital'. This occurs not so much at the level of representation but has to do 'with modes of expression that involve not only language but also heterogeneous semiotic levels' (Guattari and Rolnik 2008, 39). Laymert Garcia dos Santos, for example, made the point that the media constitute a reflective wall

> that ceaselessly proposes models of images to which the receiver can conform – images of unity, images of rationality, images of legitimacy, images of justice, images of beauty, images of scientificity. The mass media speak through and for individuals. (Laymert Garcia dos Santos in Guattari and Rolnik 2008, 78)

We see so many frightened faces loom up on our screens for example, especially through 'the news'. To return to the opening quote of this chapter: 'There is at some moment a calm and restful world. Suddenly a frightened face looms up [...]' (Deleuze and Guattari 1994, 17). These faces 'want to convince us that we are heading to some kind of disaster' (Guattari and Rolnik 2008, 66). Not only journalists and the mass media in general, but politicians especially, are particularly adept in using the 'feedback element of the affect system' in relation to fear (Angel and Gibbs 2006, 35). Images (and sounds and words) of disaster and catastrophe; images of refugees drowning in the ocean; images of a strange man speaking to a child; the image, and the language, of a lone shark that is 'stalking' the beaches; the image of a car with new and better safety features; the image of a happy person eating vegetables; 'Buy now! Don't miss out!'; the image of a person sneezing as part of an advertisement to sell yet another brand of cold and flu tablets – I already feel an itch in my throat ... Has the ad made me sick? A whole media industry is devoted to the production of an objectless fear, only to effect a positive feedback loop that produces only more fear, and the longer the source of that fear is not identified the more likely that fear will be reproduced as a general anxiety disorder (Tomkins in Angel and Gibbs 2006, 33). Capitalism, of course, proceeds precisely through this disorder (Massumi 2009).

The image of an explosion: the War on Terror. A war of affect. Enter the face of the political leader, the President or the Prime Minister as the face of the government. A face of calmness, a face of concern, a sensible face, a reliable face, the face of a father's concern, the face of a father's authority. Above all, that image functions precisely as a face in Deleuze's sense of the affection-image. The expression of the leader's face does not represent the affects, 'rather [it] becomes an agent for a range of affects produced in relation to those [it] expresses' (Angel and Gibbs 2006, 28). The face of the political leader in this way functions no differently from that of a landscape containing cows happily grazing on green grass under a blue sky – do you have organic meat for sale? The face of the government, the face of any politician, functions no differently from that of the image of a logo or a brand, or, for that matter, the image of the family, the image of the aspirational voter, the image of the terrorist, the image of the illegal immigrant, the image of what is un-American, un-Australian (Angel and Gibbs 2006, 31). As Guattari already noted:

> One of the essential tasks of the media consists in continuously adjusting facial formulas, calculating them in order to answer for every possible situation. In other words, these institutional facialities will have to 'fit in' with one another: the faciality of the average Frenchman, for example, will have to be opposed to that of the foreigner, without going to the point of a deadly racism [...] (Guattari 2011a, 91)

In such a context we are increasingly faced with a reduction of the political debate to the image and the slogan. Be alert, but not alarmed; report anything suspicious, no matter how trivial it may seem; keep an eye on your neighbour; keep an eye on your children – institute your faciality machine. Oil it well; don't cease production; become more productive, 'like a pig in a cage on antibiotics' (Radiohead 1997). More to the point, when images are facialised, they come to function as totems:

it is now up to the mass-media to produce substitute ritual and totemic facialities [...] It is no longer a territory, a clan, or an ethnicity, but the whole visual and auditory space which is implied by the standardised models of an essentially functional faciality. (Guattari 2011a, 83)

As Angel and Gibbs reiterate: 'The media generate or at least proliferate totems, figures which organise social relations through the production of empathic correlations' (Angel and Gibbs 2006, 31). In this way, the 'language of politics is increasingly reduced to the genres of the visual advertisement and the thirty-second sound byte, short promotional events based on a strategic display of product' (2006, 29). This is why the smart politician

uses low intensity positive emotion to put the electorate to sleep. Displays of negative affect, on the other hand, seem more consonant with a leadership role, and tend to connote authority, so long as the negative affect does not reach too intense a level of arousal. Contempt, for example, functions as an assertion of superiority: it is seen as more convincing and more persuasive than distress, which may be perceived as more sincere, or more genuine than contempt, which lends itself to recognition *as* display. (Angel and Gibbs 2006, 31)

We see faciality in operation throughout the media. It is in operation in celebrity, for example, not simply with respect to people who are famous for a particular thing they do or have done, such as a football star, a movie star, a pop star, but even individuals who are famous for being famous, such as Paris Hilton. Their smiles, pouts, mysterious looks, seductive eyes, naked legs can be seen on a range of products.

As noted above, much of social media has faciality as its very founding and operating principle. Again, Facebook is emblematic of this, with its particular construction of identity. Facebook even coded faciality's selective function of the binary relation 'yes or no', 'like or dislike'. In some of the social media organised around the 'interest' of dating, the selective function of faciality is even more explicitly built in: accept or reject – I don't like your face. Then there is the selfie, but also the use of images and clips, as well as quotes from written texts, that people use in constructing their various profiles, sites and blogs on social media. Sites such as LinkedIn, but also dating sites, for example, are perfect instantiations of David Byrne's line 'I am just an advertisement. For a version of myself' (Byrne 1993). In this context, images in social media, and our image world more generally, function as nothing other than clichés:

> [clichés] circulate in the external world, but [...] also penetrate each of us and constitute or internal world, so that everyone possesses only psychic clichés by which we think and feel, are thought and felt, being ourselves one cliché among others in the world that surrounds us. (Smith in Deleuze 2003, xxiii)

Indeed, according to Deleuze, we 'are besieged by photographs that are illustrations, by newspapers that are narrations, by cinema images, by television images. There are psychic clichés just as there are physical clichés – ready-made perceptions, memories, phantasms' (Deleuze 2003, 72). Worse, yet, '[n]ot only has there been a multiplication of images of every kind, around us and in our heads, but even the reactions against clichés are creating clichés. Even abstract painting has not been the last to produce its own clichés' (Deleuze 2003, 73).

A more specific problem that Deleuze identifies here is that all of us think by way of a particular type of image above all, and this is the photographic image. As he states:

> The photograph 'creates' the person or the landscape in the sense that we say the newspaper creates the event (and is not content to narrate it). What we see, what we perceive are photographs. *The most significant thing about the photograph is that it forces upon us the 'truth' of implausible and doctored images.* (Deleuze 2003, 74 [emphasis added])

Photographs 'impose themselves upon sight and rule over the eye completely' (Deleuze 2003, 75). This particular type of image '*reign[s] over vision*' (Deleuze 2003, 12) (emphasis original). The photograph, above all images perhaps, is central to the unconscious production of subjectivity. The photograph, and images in general, is a part of our dreams, 'when we daydream, when we fantasise, when we fall in love, and so on' (Guattari and Rolnik 2008, 23).

Of course, this close connection between subjectivity or individuality and in particular photography should come as no surprise.

As Romanyshyn (1989) establishes, the frame, that window that is the screen, is immediately implicated in the production of subjectivity, and particularly individuality, in a number of significant ways. For one thing, the frame is essential to the technique of linear perspective, and by extension to photography and film (Romanyshyn 1989); Alberti, in his elaboration on the technique of linear perspective, instructed us to regard the rectangular frame as a window through which we could look upon the world. As Romanyshyn (1989) argues, the frame is deeply implicated in our vision of ourselves as individuals, as well as our vision of the world. The very notion of having a unique perspective, a unique point of view as an individual, is implicated with the frame, and finds its culmination in the camera. This window establishes us as singular subjects, separate from the world, and gazing upon a world that is both subject and object.

The issue for Deleuze is precisely that we think through these images, and in particular through the frame and the photograph. Guattari points out, for example, that punks 'are polluted by images from film and television, the extent to which they incorporate a certain representation of the star system, a whole ego ideal' (Guattari and Rolnik 2008, 72). Hipsters in that regard are no different. Much that is social media instantiates something else in this respect, or rather makes more obvious what was already the case. Certainly, we operate largely by way of clichés. We can also see this with sites such as Tumblr and Instagram. These sites are largely constructed through clichés. They might be images of landscapes, a shot of a classic wave in Fiji, an image of a bottle of whisky, an image of a couple kissing, a selfie in a range of situations, an image of someone's friends, lover or child, the image of two hands holding each other, the clip of Clint Eastwood's line 'You gotta ask yourself one question: Do I feel lucky? Well, do ya, punk?' In all of these the black hole/white wall system is at work, even if only as one component of an image.

There is, of course, another form of capture going on, or rather it is the same capture but perhaps on a different register. These social media are not 'free'. When we look at social media it is clear that the economy of desire and the political economy are very much the same economy. The images we post up, the famous quotes we repeat, the clips we link to, the friends we like, the friends we unfriend – all of this is quite literally captured, coded, by and through the faciality machine that increasingly operates through our digital machines (Guattari 2011a, 97). These machines do what Instagram's slogan promises to do: 'Capture and share the world's moments'. In much of social media especially it is quite obvious that your desire is the data-mine, and faciality, subjectivity, is the machine that both sets up the mine site and does the mining, fully implicating us in the process – we are vampires feeding on our own desire. Social media are vampire media. Guattari as well as Deleuze already noted that faciality would be increasingly computerised, automated – an automation of binary choices, 'along with every other abstract quantity of information' (Guattari 2011a, 97).

Deleuze, then, sees us 'in the world as if in a pure optical and sound situation' (Deleuze 1989, 172). Worryingly, however, 'we no longer believe in this world. We do not even believe in the events that happen to us, love, death, as if they only half-concerned us. It is not we who make cinema; it is the world which looks to us like a bad film' (Deleuze 1989, 171). More specifically, capitalism in general is not something we can believe in, because capitalism does not require belief to function (Buchanan 2008, 113). As Kafka (2008, 192) observed so poignantly, '"it is not necessary to accept everything as necessary as true, one must only accept it as necessary." "A melancholy conclusion," said K. "It turns lying into a universal principle."' Capitalism in that respect removes meaning from codes (rules, regulations, etc.), turning them purely functional, leaving a pure cynicism to operate at its core (Buchanan 2008, 112). While some such as Zizek (1994, 8–9) view that cynicism as both the problem and solution, cynicism does not provide an explanation. Cynicism, according to Deleuze, much like the notions of false consciousness and ideology, operates under the illusion that there is some 'truth' out there, and that if we were only to recognise it (false consciousness), or recognise but refuse to acknowledge it (cynicism) – 'yes, the institution I work for is crazy'; 'yes, capitalism is madness'; 'yes, the stock exchange is insane' – then the situation could be fixed and resolved (Buchanan 2008, 131). However, this schism between knowledge and action is precisely what does not exist. Rather, the task for Deleuze and Guattari is to show how 'desire and interest can travel in different and indeed conflicting directions' (Buchanan 2008, 131). Why do we desire our own repression? In such a context cynicism, the lack of belief in the world, is in fact the very real danger, because then political thought and action are done for and, even worse, cynicism effectively excuses the situation (Buchanan 2008, 131). That cynicism, that lack of belief in the world, is precisely what Foucault termed fascism.

Deleuze, however, is not entirely devoid of hope. Indeed, for Deleuze, cinema, as well as painting, is precisely well situated to reconnect us to the world. Cinema should not film the world, he argues, but it should film 'belief in this world, our link' (Deleuze 1989, 172): 'Whether we are Christians or atheists, in our universal schizophrenia, *we need reasons to believe in this world*' (Deleuze 1989, 172) (emphasis original). More specifically, it is not so much that we should believe in another or transformed world, but that:

> It is only, it is simply believing in the body. It is giving discourse to the body, and, for this purpose, reaching the body before discourses, before words, before things are named: the 'first name', and even before the first name [...] We must believe in the body, but as in the germ of life, the seed which splits open the paving-stones, [...] it is not a need to believe in something else, but a need to believe in this world, of which fools are a part. (Deleuze 1989, 172–3)

It is at this point that we can return to the face's, and the frame's, deterritorialising function. As noted above, the frame, most emblematically in the close-up, separates an image from its milieu. The face, which is always already a close-up, in the first instance deterritorialises the face from the body and from the milieu (Flaxman and Oxman 2008, 50). In this moment we have what Rushton refers to as Deleuze and Guatarri's 'exemplary' empiricism: 'when I come before another person (or object, thing, entity), I enter into a realm of possibility, of possible connections, of possible confrontations, expectations, creations; in short, I enter into possibility itself' (Rushton 2002, 228). This endless possibility, however, as Rushton explains, is channelled or circumscribed by specific possibilities, and this is precisely 'the experience of the face' (Rushton 2002, 228). In this process the world takes shape, as the face 'reduces infinite possibility to finite possibility, but in doing so, it unleashes potential' (Rushton 2002, 228). Again, any assemblage opens a universe of action. The black hole doesn't reflect, but evades meaning, and in that moment creates – it is an 'area of indetermination' (Elliot 2012, 80).

Here it is useful to return to the white wall/black hole system that constitutes face, or, as Deleuze otherwise refers to it, the reflective and the intensive poles of the face (Rushton 2002). The reflective face does just that: it reflects. This is the general effect of the face, and in all likelihood generates the question 'what is this face thinking?' (2002, 229). This face reflects, and is passive, does not transform, and is even eternal, though it has a mystery, an infinity (2002, 229). Like the face of the clock, its parts 'are subservient to the general effect of the whole' (2002, 229). The intensive face, on the other hand, is part of a series. In this case 'the whole is subservient to its parts' (2002, 230). This aspect of the face is entirely about transformation, about intensity. Hitchcock's use of montage is a useful example of this, where he demonstrates, through the same close-ups of the face of an old man, how each instantiation of the same shot is affected by its placement in a series. In Hitchcock's example there are three shots. The first shot is of the man with no smile, and the last shot is of the man's face changing to a smile. If in the first series we insert the shot of a woman and child in the middle of that series then we experience the man's face as that of a kind man; if in the second series we insert the shot of a young woman in a bikini in the middle of that sequence we experience the man's face as that of a dirty old man. It is in this way that we can observe the possibilities within a face's expression (Rushton 2002, 231). The intensive face, the black hole, is about connections and possibilities, about mutation and transformation, while the reflective face, the white wall, is immutable, it is an encounter that forces us to think (2002, 231). As Zourabachvili makes clear, 'an encounter is an affect' (2012, 72). The face is very much a building frame, a structure for affect, and in this way a site for possibility.

In any case, dismantling the face is a difficult and dangerous task, but it is only through dismantling the face that we can get 'out of the black hole of subjectivity' (Deleuze and Guattari 1987, 188). At the same time, the moment

> the empty eye of power ostracises a faciality which 'does not return to it' and which no classification, equipment, or specialist

can situate, psychological and legal metalanguages are urgently implemented to escape from the impasse. The universe of dominant significations does not tolerate any escape over which it lacks control. (Guattari 2011a, 95)

As Rolnik points out, 'the point is not to assess who has more freedom, man or woman, but to circumscribe and problematise the model that to this day permeates the figures of both man and woman' (Guattari and Rolnik 2008, 112). The aim is to find our 'black holes and white walls, know them, know [our] faces' (Deleuze and Guattari 1987, 188). Only in mapping our faces might we be able to escape them.

We'll return to the question of how we might encounter something new in the following chapters, including in the context of looking at mass media as distribution machines. However, to be clear, the aim in escaping our faces is not some return to a so-called primitive state, but to avoid the organisation of a face. In this it is useful to return to Massumi's notes on the translation of *A Thousand Plateaus*, where he explains that 'to draw is an act of creation [and] [w]hat is drawn [...] does not preexist the act of drawing' (Massumi in Deleuze and Guattari 1987, xvii). It is precisely in this way that Deleuze saw both cinema and painting as more capable than photography, because the latter cannot produce a deformation in the same way the former can. In the following chapter we will focus more specifically on mass media in their function as distribution machines, and explore the possibilities for disrupting the operation of faciality in images, and for deforming the face.

CHAPTER THREE

Distribution machines

I watch TV like everybody else, I'm just as dumb, no question about it.

(GUATTARI IN GENOSKO 2012, 212)

Stupidity's never blind or mute.

(DELEUZE 1995, 129)

Media can be understood in a multitude of ways and, depending on the assemblages they form and help constitute, they often perform different functions. In this respect it is useful to consider the operation of more traditional media in their function as distribution machines. It is clear that different media affect that distribution in different ways, which in turn affects the 'thing' we think of as content. Indeed, the very act of reproducing something, such as an image or sound, can dramatically affect the status of that image or sound, and does so on different levels. As Deleuze, referring to David Hume's thesis, wrote, *'repetition changes nothing in the object repeated, but does change something in the mind which contemplates it'* (Deleuze 1994, 70 [emphasis original]).

Equally significant in that respect, and something that clearly engages Deleuze, is Walter Benjamin's insight that the mechanical reproduction of art, as in the case of film for Benjamin, also makes that reproduction and distribution immediately political, as it has a particular relationship to the masses – what we refer to as mass or commodity culture. It is also precisely for this reason that fascism, and here Benjamin was referring to fascism in Germany in the 1930s, used film, as well as radio, for clearly political purposes (Pisters 2006, 175). It is this particular aspect, that is, the relationship between mass media or broadcast media and mass or commodity culture, that forms the initial focus of this chapter.

Obviously, in titling this chapter 'Distribution machines' we aim to keep our attention focused on what it is that media in this particular aspect of their functioning do. In placing the emphasis on the machinic, we also aim to underscore that mass or broadcast media, as indeed all media, are active, processual, assemblages. As Deleuze and Guattari frequently make clear in relation to mass media, they are productive. Significantly, they connect (with) us in particular ways, and constitute or produce what we think of as culture in particular sorts of ways. For Deleuze, as well as Guattari, they are in this way deeply implicated and involved in a particular mass production of subjectivity. Mass media, indeed all media, connect us, assemble us if you like, in particular and different sorts of ways. That process of connection is not some neutral or innocent process, as should hopefully be clear by now. In particular, what concerns Deleuze and Guattari is the operation of capitalism in the operation of (mass) media, and therefore its role in the production of subjectivity. Media constitute, and insert us in, particular flows of desire, and this forms a key focal point for Deleuze as well as Guattari. This is not to state that they did not see possibilities in mass media such as radio and TV, which are explored towards the end of this chapter, but both considered it unlikely. Instead, Deleuze, and perhaps even more so Guattari, saw much potential in the use of narrowcasting, including with radio and television. In this respect, narrowcasting in the context of the internet might be an even more promising approach, including in terms of the differing degrees of interactivity enabled by digital media (Guattari 2011b, 49).

Deleuze is not at all positive about communication more generally. He often blames the mass media for having spread the idea that communication, that talking, is in and of itself a good thing. What concerns him equally is that many often perceive there to be a problem when people are not talking or are not expressing their views. As he states, '[t]he sorriest couples are those where the woman can't be preoccupied or tired without the man saying "What's wrong? Say something ..." or the man, without the woman saying ... and so on' (Deleuze 1995, 129). It is precisely this spirit, as he terms it, that radio and television have spread everywhere. Consequently, 'we're riddled with pointless talk, insane quantities of words and images' (1995, 129). As noted in the previous chapter, these form part of a general visual and sound-scape composed of so many clichés, and clichés of clichés (Deleuze 2003), that media, whether print, radio, TV, or, indeed, social media or any other media, are involved in the transmission of. He equally saw cinema involved in 'the dark organisation of cliches, [participating] in their fabrication and propagation, as much as magazines and television' (Deleuze 1986, 214).

At times Deleuze is particularly critical of television as a medium. He not only accuses it of threatening death to cinema (and a first death of cinema he attributes to radio), but considers it 'the form in which the new powers of "control" become immediate and direct' (Deleuze 1995, 75). In short, it is clear that for Deleuze there is something very profound at work in television, as well as radio, as mediums. As media, they clearly function in a way that is qualitatively different from other media:

> one is subjected to TV insofar as one uses and consumes it, in the very particular situation of a subject of the statement that more or less mistakes itself for a subject of enunciation ('you, dear television viewers, who make TV what it is ...'); the technical machine is the medium between two subjects. But one is enslaved by TV as a human machine insofar as the television viewers are no longer consumers or users, nor even subjects who supposedly 'make' it, but intrinsic component pieces, 'input' and 'output', feedback or recurrences that are no longer connected to the machine in such a way as to produce or use it. In machinic enslavement, there is nothing but transformations and exchanges of information, some of which are mechanical, others human. The term 'subjection', of course, should not be confined to the national aspect, with enslavement seen as international or worldwide. (Deleuze and Guattari 1987, 458–9)

Of course, as Deleuze makes clear elsewhere, a medium, nor for that matter any technological device or machines, cannot be under-stood in and of by itself: 'the machines don't explain anything, you have to analyse the collective arrangements of which the machines are just one component' (Deleuze 1995, 175). In short, we have to consider television's, as well as radio's, function as part of the assemblages, the 'collective arrangements' they operate in and as, and function as part of. In this way, we need to consider what it is that television and radio, as well as other media, as machines for distributing so-called content, *do*, including and especially in terms of their economic and, therefore, social operation.

Taking such a view, if we briefly consider the rise to power of Hitler in the 1930s, propaganda and mass media were precisely productive if we use Deleuze's approach. Here it is useful to briefly return to Deleuze's conceptualisation of the virtual. One view, for example, might be that what made the National Socialists successful is that they made actual what was already virtual in people's minds – the National Socialists simply activated already existing ideas. However, this is a misunderstanding of Deleuze's notion of the virtual (Rushton 2002, 226–7), because such an explanation continues to rely on a model of communication and thought that relies on the notion of a copy and an original, that is, a representational model. Taking Deleuze's conceptualisation of the virtual, it is not the case that Hitler and the National Socialists somehow enabled a more accurate or truer representation of what were already pre-existing ideas and feelings (Rushton 2002, 227). Instead, Hitler and the National Socialists made it possible, created the possibility, for 'a myth of German greatness (of powerful leadership, the master race, the Jewish conspiracy, and so on)' (Rushton 2002, 227). In this way, Hitler did not actualise already existing feelings, but, as we explored in relation to faciality in the previous chapter, virtualised them, created the possibility for their coming into existence. In different words, he constituted a particular assemblage. As Deleuze and Guattari state: 'Hitler got the fascists sexually aroused. Flags, nations, armies, banks get a lot of people aroused' (Deleuze and Guattari 1983, 293).

A different example might be the occasional story we see on the news, or in some current affairs programme, televising a report on a ballet programme being introduced in a primary school. In this particular example, the school is in a remote desert community, and the children are very young. It's likely that many of these children will have no preconception of what ballet is, and in that respect might not see ballet as somehow a gendered activity. They all participate in the exercises and seem to have a great time. Yet at the end the teacher comments on how well the boys did. This immediately codes the activity of ballet for the children: 'Ah, so boys normally don't do this, but I'm a boy!' The code is then repeated by the reporter – 'and even the boys did it'. There is for the children here not an actualisation of a particular thought or feeling – who knew there was this thing called 'ballet' and that 'only girls do it' – but rather a virtualisation, a coding, at work, so that the next time they do ballet they can say 'But boys aren't meant to do ballet!' This 'framing', the coding of an imperial semiotic, is emblematic of what broadcast media distribute.

A critical point to make here is that Deleuze and Guattari propose a general theory of society in terms of 'a generalized theory of flows' (Deleuze and Guattari 1983, 262), and specifically in terms of understanding the relationship between what they refer to as social production and desire. As Smith (2011) points out, when we consider society at a variety of levels, and, indeed, life in general, it is composed of an extraordinary variety of flows. The flow of water, the flow of information, the flow of money, the flow of air, flows of people, flows of refugees. More to the point for Deleuze and Guattari, 'there is desiring-production from the moment there is social production'(Deleuze and Guattari 1983, 139). In short, what they term desire is not defined in the manner that Freud defines, as some lack, but as something, a flow, that is precisely productive, and is, in fact, precisely productive of society and the institutions that it consists of. This is something we can see in the simplest examples, including the regulation of the flow of water (Smith 2011, 37). But this can also be observed just as much with flows of money (taxation) or flows of people (borders). As Smith points out in relation to media, for example:

> One can even think of flows of thought, and the attempt to code and control the flow of thought via marketing, advertising, the media, and so on (such as the flow of scientific knowledge, as well as a flow of stupidity and opinion). (Smith 2011, 38)

We will examine marketing and advertising, as well as news, and its involvement in the coding of desire in more detail later in the book, but the key point that Deleuze and Guattari make is that it is the job of any society to regulate, contain and code desire. Indeed, it is 'the business of the socius' (Deleuze and Guattari 1983, 139).

However, what distinguishes capitalism from other forms of society, that is, 'precapitalist social machines' (1983, 139), is that capitalism 'is the only social machine that is constructed on the basis of decoded flows' (1983, 139). Capitalism is the only form of social organisation that 'liberates the flows of desire' from social codes (1983, 139), though it does this under specific conditions whereby those flows are immediately recoded. In this, Deleuze and Guattari rely on Marx's insight that:

> [Smith and Ricardo] located the essence of wealth, not in its object (land or money), but rather in an abstract subjective essence, which is my *labour capacity*, or my capacity to produce. What faith is to religion, labour is to political economy: humans produce gods in the same way they produce Prell shampoo or Ford automobiles. (Smith 2011, 39)

In this way capitalism decoded, deterritorialised, slave labour and serfdom to produce 'free labour', and deterritorialised wealth, which now is no longer tied to land, but is a 'pure, homogenous and independent *capital*' (Smith 2011, 39). This, Deleuze and Guattari argue, is similar to what Freud did in relation to desire and the unconscious, when he recognised that the essence of desire was not found in relation to other objects or other aims, but that it was an abstract as well as a subjective essence (Smith 2011, 39). The significant move that Deleuze and Guattari then make is that they view the political economy and the libidinal economy as the same economy:

> our impulses and affects, and even our unconscious drives, what seems to be the most individual and personal part of ourselves (libidinal economy), are themselves immediately part of what Marx called the economic infrastructure, that is, the material base of every social formation (political economy). In other words, it is impossible to posit a mental or psychic reality to desire that is different from the material reality of social production. (Smith 2011, 39–40)

In short, to return to the example of Hitler and the National Socialists above, it is not the case that people were somehow duped, or that they were blinded by ideology in some way, but that people actually desired this. They desired, or rather, produced, assembled, their own repression: 'It is not an ideological problem, a problem of failing to recognise [...] It is a problem of desire, *and desire is part of the infrastructure*' (Deleuze and Guattari 1983, 104).

For example, if we briefly turn to the so-called climate change debate, no amount of scientific evidence is going to somehow unveil the truth of the situation to so many of our politicians or so-called 'leaders of industry'. We see that they are refusing to act in any concerted manner – 'Why don't they do something, can't they see something is going wrong?' However, this applies just as much to our politicians as it applies to us. We will continue to drive our cars, switch on the air conditioning, watch our plasma screens, because on some level that is precisely what we desire, much like the humans in the movie *Wall-E*, plugged into their chairs and entertainment screens and devices. In short, desire, the unconscious, 'our impulses and drives, always constitute a social field – are always arranged by (our) social formations, including in the sense that we desire our own repression' (Savat and Thompson 2015, 285). Our 'interests' in that respect, in a similar way to our faces as we argued in the previous chapter, are not our own. Rather, our interests are particular codifications of (the flow of) desire, and marketing and advertising are focused on producing these codes. Our world is the way it is because we desire it this way:

> Repressing desire, not only for others but in oneself, being the cop for others and for oneself – that is what arouses, and it is not ideology, it is economy ... A violence without purpose, a joy, a pure joy in feeling oneself a wheel in the machine, traversed by flows, broken by schizzes. Placing oneself in a position where one is thus traversed, broken, fucked by the socius, looking for the right place where, according to the aims and the interests assigned to us, one feels something moving that has neither an interest nor a purpose. A sort of art for art's sake in the libido, a taste for a job well done, each one his own place, the banker, the cop, the soldier, the technocrat, the bureaucrat, and why not the worker, the trade-unionist. Desire is agape. (Deleuze and Guattari 1983, 346–7)

Indeed, according to Deleuze and Guattari, mass media in particular play a large role in that codification of the flow of desire. As Gary

Genosko reminds us, for Guattari TV was 'an intense experience of territorialisation' (Genosko 2012, 212). For Guattari, as for Deleuze:

> Mass culture produces individuals: standardised individuals, linked to one another in accordance with hierarchical systems, value systems, systems of submission – not visible, explicit systems of submission, as in animal ethology, or as in archaic or precapitalist societies. These systems of submission are much more hidden. I wouldn't say they are 'internalised' or 'interiorised', an expression [...] implying that subjectivity is something to be filled. On the contrary, it is *produced*. Not just individuated subjectivity – subjectivity of individuals – but social subjectivity that can be found at every level of production and consumption. And, what's more, an *unconscious* production of subjectivity. (Guattari and Rolnik 2008, 23 [emphasis original])

Deleuze and Guattari conceptualised this as the production of a factory, 'this huge factory, this mighty capitalistic machine', which precisely is involved in producing the images, and sounds and texts, that form part of our dreams and fantasies, 'when we fall in love, and so on' (2008, 23). In this way the machine that is capitalism occupies 'a hegemonic function in all these fields' (2008, 23). As Guattari elsewhere laments:

> We are crushed under the weight of the mass media, by images of power, by a manipulation of the imagination in the service of an oppressive social order, by the fabrication, whatever the cost, of a majority consensus, by the cult of security, by processes of intoxication that scare people about everything and nothing, infantilising them to the point that they no longer ask themselves questions. (Guattari 2009, 46)

We considered aspects of this in the chapter on image machines, and in particular the operation of the abstract machine of faciality and its central involvement in the process of subjectivation. As already considered in that chapter, the cult of security since Deleuze's and Guattari's passings has continued and in fact strengthened in ever more aspects of our day-to-day life. This is especially so when we consider the emergence and development of control society that Deleuze warned us of in his essay 'Postscript on societies of control' (Deleuze 1992). This particular machine's production has continued unabated. At the same time, and perhaps as part of that same process, we continue to experience an ever-increasing infantilisation of people. The latest evidence or instantiation of such infantilisation, for example, is found in the fact that colouring books for adults are now a big growth sector in the publishing industry, the argument being that being creative decreases anxiety and stress. There is sadly no irony in the fact that this activity is not particularly creative but rather offers a return to the 'guided creation' of childhood. We see such infantilisation, sometimes in the form of intense regulation (see Graeber 2015), in the most concerning sectors of society, ranging from the treatment of employees by managers, especially in occupational health and safety, as well as in teaching, including at universities. This goes beyond simple spoon-feeding of so-called content, and includes the expected automation of the most simple tasks. A complaint of one student, that there was a problem with a PDF document, was that the letters were too small: 'But you know you can zoom in, don't you?' 'Of course,' was the indignant response, 'but the point is that I shouldn't have to do it.' *1984* is not our model, but rather *Brave New World*, as Neill Postman pointed out in *Amusing Ourselves to Death* (1986). We believe that perhaps more people will be familiar with the kids' movie *Wall-E* – *Brave New World*'s equivalent for today's generations. Though unlike in the movie *Wall-E*, it is unlikely the revelation of some truth will cause us to act differently.

The situation today, despite, or perhaps because of, the internet and its reconfiguration of traditional broadcast and print industries, is even more desperate than it was when Deleuze and Guattari first warned us. This should come as no surprise. While the internet very clearly has a deterritorialising capacity, and uncodes flows, it is also precisely destructive in this way. This destruction is very much a key characteristic of capitalism. As Deleuze and Guattari make very clear, following Marx, capitalism precisely proceeds through a process of uncoding as part of its operation. As Smith explains (2011, 51), this is not in terms of deciphering a code or unlocking or revealing some hidden secret or meaning, but in the sense of undoing a code, uncoding a flow, creating a line of flight. This is precisely why social formations prior to capitalism so resisted capitalism, because of its decoding or uncoding capacity, that is, it proceeds by way of destruction in the first instance, as well as creation. This occurs in terms of the un/coding of a whole amalgam of flows. Marx identified many such examples, including with respect to the distribution of both people and goods in the economy:

> *Circulation proceeds in space and time.* Economically considered, the spatial condition, the bringing of the product to the market, belongs to the production process itself. The product is really finished only when it is on the market ... [T]his spatial moment is important in so far as the expansion of the market and the exchangeability of the product are connected with it. The reduction of the costs of this *real* circulation (in space) belongs to the development of the forces of production by capital, the reduction of the costs of its realisation ... *Secondly, the temporal moment.* This is an essential part of the concept of circulation... The abbreviation of this moment is likewise development of productive force. (Marx 1973, 533–4)

While for Marx the railway was one key instrument in reducing the spatial condition, as well as the temporal moment, resulting precisely in the destruction of a particular conceptualisation space-time, including the spaces 'in-between' (Schivelbusch 1986), and so destroying the flow between some points, for us today it is the internet that serves a similar function. The internet proceeds precisely temporally rather than spatially – no movement, but pure speed (Virilio 1986), pure flow, of which foreign exchange traders are in some way exemplary (Knorr Cetina and Preda 2007). The internet operates precisely as a distribution machine that shortens the spatial condition to near-zero, and abbreviates the temporal moment to the point where global financial institutions operate in terms of nano-seconds. Their distance from the server has to be regulated, the flows of the different companies curtailed so as to produce a level playing field. The internet produces a shrinking as well as a stretching of time, with some playing on a very different time. This shrinking and stretching of time precisely belongs to the production process itself. We don't need to only refer to foreign exchange traders' sense of time (Knorr Cetina and Preda 2007) to come up with examples. We experience it when we play Massive Multiple Online Role-Playing Games (MMORPG) and players are differentiated in terms of a time lag measured in milliseconds – the sense that you are always somehow 'moving' just that fraction of a second slower than someone else, no matter how fast you might react. The speed of flow and not the movement of flow is what matters with digital media, with the flow of information – different flow rates, as well as differing viscosities, the resistance to change of a flow, comparable to the deformation of solid forms. In this regard the internet, digital media, deals with very different flows: not the flows of amorphous solids, like the flow of refugees, or the sand on a beach, but fluids. Nonetheless, still desire, and desire uncoded, as well as a whole different way to recode desire, to capture desire. From crowdsourcing to data-mining, being able to see 'the scene' – a streetscape, a face, a population – for 'what it is'. Showing the 'hidden' information in the world, the flows around us, though from a Deleuzian approach, this is precisely about the virtualisation of new flows of desire – new profits to be made. Thanks to our mobile phones, we carry the market in our pocket, always at the marketplace now, just as the market taps ever more directly in our heads now, discovering those 'hidden patterns', the flowlines and streamlines of information, even when we know they are precisely not hidden, but created, assembled, virtualised, produced by a variety of abstract machines that find their operation in our media. In this regard there is a whole different history to be done of media flows as viscous media and media viscosity: print-based media clearly have a higher viscosity than social media, for example (Savat 2013).

While there is an argument to be made that the increased use of digital media has challenged broadcast media in some ways, it should be immediately clear that the processes of which both Deleuze and Guattari spoke in relation to mass media have not diminished. What we are very much seeing is what Bolter and Grusin term remediation (Bolter and Grusin 2000). We would argue that, if anything, the process of subjectification has increased in both scope and intensity as part and parcel of that remediation. In some respects this is further evidence of Deleuze and Guattari's claim that the systems of submission they write and speak of are not so much internalised or somehow imposed on us, but that subjectivity, both individuated and social, is precisely found at 'every level of production and consumption' (Guattari and Rolnik 2008, 23), and that the production of subjectivity is precisely unconscious (Deleuze and Guattari 1983). Stated differently, the production of both an individuated and social subjectivity that so troubled Deleuze, as well as Guattari, is just as evident through the internet as it is in broadcast or mass media. As Buchanan (2009) points out, the jury is still very much out as to whether the internet is a rhizome, despite uncritical claims by many that the internet is an example of a rhizome. If it is a rhizome we should keep in mind that rhizomes are neither inherently 'good' or 'bad', and nor are deterritorialisation or reterritorialisation necessarily 'good' or 'bad'. Rather, any degree of 'goodness' is a function of the assemblage, and how the components shift in relation to each other. The new territories we form are 'just as capable of nourishing a modern fascism as of freeing a revolutionary charge' (Deleuze and Guattari 1983, 258). Deleuze and Guattari repeat these messages throughout their work.

Part of how Deleuze and Guattari suggest we proceed is by way of their method of schizoanalysis. One key component of this is to analyse how a particular machine, a particular assemblage, works. It is to examine what the components are, as well as how they function in relation to each other. As Deleuze and Guattari explain in their *Anti-Oedipus*, part of the method and process of schizo-analysis involves that of taking on the role of a mechanic (Deleuze and Guattari 1983, 322). If we briefly return to the chapter on the assemblage, this can and should involve a whole range of components. It also means questioning how particular beliefs function as part of an assemblage. While in *Anti-Oedipus* the emphasis is on the Freudian focus on Oedipus, it goes beyond this. For example, it can begin by examining something as seemingly simple as the word 'culture'. As Guattari demonstrates, when we examine the operation of mass culture and its mass production of particular forms of subjectivity, and in particular individuality, culture functions as a bit of a trick word, a '[barrier-notion] that prevent us from understanding the reality of the processes in question' (Guattari and Rolnik 2008, 23).

Obviously, there are different ways in which we can understand the use the of the word 'culture'. Culture can refer to a notion of cultivation, for example, such as 'cultivating the mind' (Guattari and Rolnik 2008, 23–4). This use of the word culture is associated with a value judgement as to what constitutes culture or what can be considered cultural, and what is not. For example, the work from people such as Adorno (2002) and others in the Frankfurt School operates with a sense of what constitutes high culture and what constitutes low culture or no culture. So-called mass culture, in the case of people such as Adorno and Horkheimer (1997), is considered low culture. Deleuze too is at times accused of operating with just such a sense of culture in his *Cinema* books by some, because he mostly refers to avant-garde and experimental films and film-makers, while ignoring the popular and commercially successful.

Another use of the word culture treats it as 'synonymous with civilisation' (Guattari and Rolnik 2008, 23). This use of the word culture grants everything and everyone the status of having culture. It is what we refer to when we speak of people having a particular cultural identity, that is, in this use of the word culture everyone has culture. There is no such thing as not having culture. It can refer to a person's sense of national identity, or regional identity, or what 'tribe' a person feels part of. It can find its expression, as Guattari and Rolnik (2008) point out, both in notions of race, as in the case of the National Socialists and Hitler in Germany, as well as in freedom movements.

Mass culture, however, for both Deleuze and Guattari, refers to commodity culture. This is the form of culture that refers to 'everything that contributes to the production of semiotic objects (such as books and films), distributed in a particular market of monetary circulation or in the state sector. This culture is disseminated in the same way as Coca-Cola, cigarettes, cars, or anything else' (Guattari and Rolnik 2008, 24). In this case, culture 'is the production and distribution of cultural goods', and is a culture that 'is constantly produced, reproduced, and modified' (2008, 26). This form of culture can also be measured, 'according to data concerning the number of books produced, the number of films, or the number of cultural venues' (2008, 26). Especially in the context of so-called Big Data it should be immediately obvious how this sort of measuring is even more extreme today. It can be seen in something as seemingly innocuous as how many 'likes' a YouTube clip or Facebook page has, to how many times a particular journal article has been downloaded, to how many times a person's work has been cited and by whom, to how many times a student logged on to the 'Learning Management System' in a week, and what texts he or she clicked on and read in that week. As we noted above, a whole new range of patterns, flows of information, can be 'discovered', that is, set loose and captured. As our managers tell us, this will be good for us.

While the 'production of the means of mass communication [...] generates a culture with a universal vocation' (Guattari and Rolnik 2008, 27), it tolerates forms of subjectivity, or rather 'subjective territories', that are not part of it. Stated differently, while there is the production, through mass media, of a more universal capitalistic subjectivity, there is not simply an acceptance of so-called minority cultures and subjectivities or territories on the margins, but capitalism itself produces new margins, new subjective territories: 'individuals, families, social groups, minorities, and so on' (2008, 27). Capitalism often allows and aims to produce precisely what is outlandish, that is, deterritorialising, precisely so that it can be captured or coded, and come to function for both value exchange (cultural and economic) and profit. Even culture jamming has been captured through this process (Buchanan 2008, 26).

Of course, the word tolerance, while suggesting an acceptance of different views and different ways of existing, also at the same time suggests that in principle you do not agree with those views. Stated differently, the 'industrialisation of the production of culture' through mass media, as well as ministries of culture in their various guises, is not some innocent or neutral process, even if people and organisations express that they value everyone's culture. As Guattari and Rolnik explain:

> Culture is not merely the transmission of cultural information, the transmission of systems of modelisation; it's also a way for the capitalistic elites to exhibit what I would call a general market of power. This is not only a power over cultural objects, or over the possibilities of handling them and creating something, but also a power to attribute cultural objects to oneself as a distinctive sign in one's social relations with others. (Guattari and Rolnik 2008, 28)

The example that Guattari provides here is to compare some banal statement that a person, say a teacher or student, might make in the context of a conversation about a well-known author in the context of an everyday conversation, with that same statement being made by a celebrity or well-known politician on television. When the student or teacher says it in the context of an everyday conversation the statement doesn't affect that person's status and value within their social field in the same way as when a well-known celebrity or politician makes that very same statement about that same well-known author on television (Guattari and Rolnik 2008, 29). With the latter the effect of the distribution machine is that it marks them as a particular type of person, that is, as belonging to 'the field of culture', a 'field of power' (2008, 29). The so-called content of the statement is not relevant in such contexts.

We see this power of distribution machines in operation regularly in the mass media, for example, when people aim to discredit particular people or causes. The Obama administration's Iran nuclear deal, announced in July 2015, is widely supported by the world's most knowledgeable experts on nuclear arms and weapons control (Timm 2015), yet somehow the advice of these experts is entirely ignored by those opposing the deal. Even more telling is the earlier noted public debate around climate change and global warming. Again, what matters here is not the truth, the unveiling of the truth, but the particular assemblage that is at work, the coding of desire as a particular interest. Another example is where we might see a journalist report on, for example, artificial intelligence and robots, aiming to create some anxiety around the idea that robots will one day take over, even though the various experts who are interviewed for the story all state this idea is very far from being realised and we certainly won't see it in the coming decades, if ever, yet in the end the reporter still focuses on the fear, the anxiety. Perhaps the reporter didn't watch *Wall-E*, where artificial intelligence saves us from our humanity.

Another example in which we can see that content is not what we should focus on in the first instance, but rather how something works, is clear in the figure of the shark, which so pervades our media. Facts are entirely irrelevant, that is, it matters little to most people that more deaths occur from bee stings, work accidents, stress or car accidents. Indeed, these causes of death we seem to simply take in our stride, as part of the everyday scene – it would be almost unusual not to have these as part of the daily media diet. But a shark attack has a different resonance, a different function in that regard. The fear provoked by the figure of the shark is precisely what we desire (Buchanan 2008, 77). Just as in the movie *Jaws*, which follows the narrative of the Western, the figure of the shark presents a 'common enemy' that enables us 'to come together without having to renounce individual interest' (Buchanan 2008, 78). In other words, the shark produces 'community spirit' in much the same way that 'the terrorist' produces community spirit. It is precisely this that we also see in disaster movies and images of catastrophe in general, even when, as in the case of the aftermath of Hurricane Katrina, community spirit is precisely what seemed to be lacking, especially on the part of political leaders and officials (Levine 2015). Indeed, perhaps that very image itself, the image of the dysfunctional politician, the actual dysfunctional politician, is precisely what we desire. After all, despite continuous and never-ending complaints about the people we elect for office, clearly so many continually re-elect the same people, the same political parties, because these are precisely the politicians and the policies we desire, because on some level we want more of the same. In that respect, the images of the dysfunctional politician, shark, earthquake, hurricane are precisely functioning as a cliché and therefore precisely what prevents the genesis of the new, 'just as opinion and convention prevent the genesis of thought' (Smith in Deleuze 2003, xxiii). This suggests that the materiality of the distribution machine is less relevant than the social assemblage that expresses it: that is, the media we have are the media we desire, and the internet alone is not sufficient to change that.

Again, we need to consider the operation of affect in such situations. Politicians, advertisers and marketers know very well how this functions. Most tellingly, one of Australia's Prime Ministers was very effective with a small number of slogans, most notable of which was 'stop the boats'. At one point, he was asked by a journalist how he thought the economy had improved when all the economic figures suggested the opposite, to which he responded, 'Well, we've stopped boats'. Perhaps this was a slogan used one too many times, as he was forced to resign by his own party the following week. In short, as Deleuze and Guattari make clear, it is not actually the competence of political leaders or experts or scientists that is at issue. A person's competence, including the so-called content of his or her statements, has little to no impact on public opinion as it is produced through the mass media. This was a point that others already made well before Deleuze and Guattari, as, for example, McLuhan pointed out in one of the first televised presidential debates, Nixon–Kennedy. On radio Nixon was considered the better candidate, but on TV Kennedy was considered so (McLuhan 1964, 329–30). Indeed, knowledge or expertise resides less in the person, but rather in complex systems or assemblages of modern image management and administration (Guattari and Rolnik 2008). Instead, what is more significant is how culture functions as 'a quantity of information', and specifically how culture is distributed.

In this respect, one key problem Deleuze and Guattari have with mass media and the way 'culture' operates as a substance through which and by which subjectivity is produced is that the mass media, including governments, predominantly don't see 'culture' as either political or social. Instead governments 'distribute culture for consumption, in the same way that minimum food rations are distributed in some societies' (Guattari and Rolnik 2008, 32). 'I watched five YouTube clips today, and read one chapter – I consumed some culture.' Indeed, any overt so-called 'politicisation' of culture is often immediately and strictly dealt with, either by suppressing it in some form, or by in some way normalising it, that is, making it match the dominant subjectivity. For example, Adam Goodes, a well-known football player in Australia, at one of his matches made an overt display of his 'culture', his aboriginality. This triggered a debate precisely around the word culture – he was exhibiting a different culture, yet that very performance of a different culture was also read as an overt political and divisive act. It was precisely creative in that he was clearly deforming the White Man face, less waves of 'sameness' than the White Man face, opening the black holes of subjectivity. The consequence was that he could not play the following week, as he received an intense negative reaction in the media and from 'the public'. We all 'like' culture, we all 'like' 'common sense', except when it is no longer the culture of The Same, because it is precisely at such moments that a line of flight might eventuate, a flow might become uncoded, and be released. This is precisely why culture today, as well as common sense, is catastrophic for Deleuze, as well as Guattari (2011b). As Buchanan explains:

> desiring-production is that aspect of desire which if it were to pass into social production and reproduction would sow the seeds of disorder and revolution as it does every time a little piece of it manages to elude the coding society imposes on it so as to contain it. (Buchanan 2008, 45)

It is in this way that we need to approach Deleuze and Guattari's view that there is no such thing as 'popular culture' or 'high culture', but only 'capitalistic culture, which permeates all fields of social expression' (Guattari and Rolnik 2008, 33), and which codes the production of subjectivity in increasingly more and more aspects of life, including non-human life. It is also precisely because of the manner in which culture operates, through the media-sphere, that Deleuze and Guattari advocate analysing the collective arrangements, rather than a specific object or field:

> [I]t is necessary to create a wider concept of collective equip-ments, one that would encompass all media and systems of transportation. The theory of assemblages, as I propose it, no longer allows us to think about collective equipments in the usual way, that is, independently from productive forces, and the training systems of the collective labor force. It implies the existence of a continuum between domains that, until [recently], had been the privilege either of state apparatuses or of the private sector, or even of private life. (Guattari 2011b, 47)

This continuum, for Deleuze and Guattari, is precisely constituted, at least in part, by the variety of media we use. This does not just apply to so-called mass or broadcast media, but also digital media. Indeed, digital media, the internet, is reaching a point that, as Eric Schmidt, Google's chairman and ex-CEO, stated, it will disappear:

> There will be so many IP addresses ... so many devices, sensors, things that you are wearing, things that you are interacting with that you won't even sense it. *It will be part of your presence all the time.* Imagine you walk into a room, and the room is dynamic. And with your permission *and all of that*, you are interacting with the things going on in the room. (Schmidt in Smith 2015 [emphasis added])

Of course the internet, as Mark Poster (2001) pointed out, has interconnectedness as its very principle of operation. While Guattari argues that besides 'mass media' the 'social resources, resources for health, education, leisure', as well as 'modern means of transportation', are critical in the formation of that continuum, it should be immediately clear that 'the internet' pervades all these areas, which is precisely Schmidt's point. It ranges from our cars, to our mobiles, to our books, to our classrooms, to our TVs, our fridges, our billboards, our clothes, and so on. Increasingly, despite Schmidt's rather offhand statement 'and with your permission and all that', we will have no choice but to participate – that choice disappeared some time ago now. Media are so deeply implicated, and instituted, in our day-to-day life, and in the production of our subjectivity. What is concerning is the continuum's relation to the productive forces, that is, capitalism. As Deleuze states: 'Maybe speech and communication have been corrupted. They're thoroughly permeated by money – and not by accident but by their very nature' (Deleuze 1995, 175). This continuum that media are productive of, through the procedure of distribution, and in particular 'the internet', the media through which we live our day-to-day life, by which we now 'participate' in life, is nothing other than a culture in which a particular organism is cultured, that is, produced.

Both Deleuze and Guattari wrote less on digital media and the internet. On the one hand, it was clear to Deleuze (1992) that digital media were part of the production of a new kind of society: control society. As Deleuze suggested in his brief postscript on control societies, we were no longer a disciplinary society, and media, computers, were a clear expression of this. No longer individuals, but, even worse, dividuals: the individual's identity constantly postponed, constantly divided against itself, a pure flow of information, and as such precisely formless, flow, fluid, pure information (Savat 2013). By way of digital media it is immediately clear how we, our actions and thoughts, are constituted as code, as pure information – information to be manipulated, to be extracted, mined – that is, to be sold. As long as media are permeated by money, this is unlikely to change. It is clear that in much of social media, as was the case with television and radio, we, that is, the flows of information that we generate, are precisely the commodity that is packaged and sold. We are no longer even customers, as Deleuze laments (Deleuze 1995, 153–64). The customers are other companies, other corporations. Print and magazines established this basic principle, and radio, TV and now 'the internet', from Facebook to YouTube, simply copy the same models (Monaco 2009). As Morozov (2015) points out, Google is simply an advertising machine. In short, mass media has less to do with the materiality of the media device and more about the assemblage it operates as a component in, that is, capitalism. It matters little in that respect that 'the screen's no longer a window or a door (behind which ...) nor a frame or a surface (in which ...) but a computer screen on which images as "data" slip around' (Deleuze 1995, 76).

There is, of course, also cause for hope. The media device in itself does not necessarily prevent something new, something different, from emerging, from escaping. As assemblages they constitute precisely a universe of action. Stated differently, what we need to recognise, as explained in relation to assemblages, is that it is not the medium in itself that is necessarily arborescent or rhizomatic. As Deleuze makes clear throughout his work, all things are arborescent and rhizomatic *to a degree*, and whether something is rhizomatic or arborescent at any given moment is dependent on a variety of factors. Certainly we can argue that the internet facilitates massive arborescent modes of thought or structures, but it, as any medium, has a capacity for something new to emerge, and the internet, at least for the time being, is more open to this than TV is. Guattari for example, is quite positive about the potential of the internet, partly because the internet can still function without gatekeepers. Indeed, as Genosko (2012) points out, the issue with TV as a medium is that '[a] ny link between television and becoming is hard to grasp for a scholarly community that has not wanted to appreciate television's potential' (Genosko 2012, 212). What we might be able to call transversal TV in that regard, following Guattari's concept of transversality, and in this way rhizomatic, in this respect does not simply mean producing some 'illusion of participation' with an audience responding via Twitter on TV, or by way of a YouTube channel, though it is entirely possible this can create lines of flight (2012, 218). More likely, notes Genosko, are experiments such as Telestreet, or the notion of the *télé-auteur*. Deleuze too acknowledged TV's potential: '[T]elevision has, potentially, just as significant an aesthetic function as any other form of expression ...' (Deleuze 1995, 72). Deleuze's point is simply that

> [TV] hasn't sought its own specific identity in an aesthetic function but in a social function, a function of control and power, the dominance of the medium shot, which denies any

exploration of perception, in the name of the professional eye. Thus any innovation that does occur may appear in some unexpected corner, some unusual situation [...] (Deleuze 1995, 72–3)

In this respect Guattari's aims with respect to TV were to create 'a counter-example that would inspire, an extraordinary television which would engage viewers as potential users and makers, in addition to providing impetus for their mobile imaginaries that move toward dismantling the artificial neurosis' (Genosko 2012, 218). In this way narrowcast, in any form, held more potential for Guattari, including in relation to radio, as in the example of mini-FM in Japan (Ueno 2012), where free radio stations could only broadcast with a radius of one kilometre (2012, 188). It should be clear, then, why he was so excited by digital media, while equally cognisant of its dangers.

Indeed, the internet has much capacity to sustain precisely the sorts of models that Guattari as well as Deleuze suggested with respect to narrowcasting. As Guattari pointed out in the context of free radio, 'The possibility of reappropriating the media, for example through free radio stations, can subvert the modelisation of subjectivity' (Guattari and Rolnik 2008, 63). Nor should we ignore aspects of so-called remix culture here. We state 'so-called' because all cultures are remix cultures (Lessig 2008), except that this is now something that needs to be pointed out to us because capitalism has so disturbingly dissociated us from the idea. We now so readily accept the idea that culture is commodified, a product to be bought and sold, to be mined. Nonetheless mass culture too is remix culture, and perhaps increasingly so again. In this way mass culture might still enable a subversion of subjectivity. Even punk, which Guattari was very much critical of in terms of the models that it reproduces, can have a vital importance for some people in this context:

Hundreds of groups live out and embody their desire in collective undertakings such as rock and punk, which for them can be of vital importance. Although they convey elements of meaning of the dominant ideology, and although they are prisoners of numerous systems of modelisation, they express [...] what I call a 'vector of molecular revolution,' which can subvert the modelisation of subjectivity. (Guattari and Rolnik 2008, 73)

This may well apply to a range of genres and styles, and the lines of escape that might operate in them: 'An escape for language, for music, for writing. What we call pop – pop music, pop philosophy, pop writing [...] To make use of the polylingualism of one's own language' (Deleuze and Guattari 1986, 26–7). In part this may be at the core of some notions of remix culture today, that '[n]evertheless, despite all the heterogeneous, mass-produced character of its components (in which everything seems to have been borrowed from the dominant oppressive systems), these components can constitute elements in a process of singularisation' (Guattari and Rolnik 2008, 73). Or, as they term it in their book on Kafka, a 'becoming-minor' (Deleuze and Guattari 1986, 73). It is important here to differentiate singularity from identity, however: 'Singularity is an existential concept, whereas identity is a concept of referentiality, of the limiting of reality to frames and reference, frames that may be imaginary' (Guattari and Rolnik 2008, 94), though these singularities are in part what capitalism aims to create and co-opt: 'For example, certain traits of singularity in black music are integrated into jazz, which is distributed throughout the social field and becomes a kind of universal music' (Guattari and Rolnik 2008, 69), which is precisely where so-called cool-hunters come into play (Buchanan 2008). In any case, as Deleuze also states in relation to creation:

[T]he operation of extracting, or extracting something doesn't happen all by itself. As McLuhan has shown, when the medium is hot, nothing circulates or communicates except through the cool, which controls every active interaction, including painter with model, spectator with painter, and model with copy. What counts is the perpetual reversals of hot and cool, according to which the hot can cool down the cool and the cool reheat the hot: it's like heating an oven with snowballs. (Deleuze 2004a, 150)

We could list countless examples in the context of digital media in which this occurs, including through the remixes of clips of movies such as the last scenes of Hitler in his bunker in the movie *Downfall*, but also Wikileaks, as well as various crowdsourcing uses, such as we see in some examples with Ushahidi. In fact, the latter enable a mapping of desire, or at least of the operation of interest, a cartography of the operations of social regimes, even if such sites simultaneously enable the mapping of the most mundane, such as the best burgers in New York. The key issue for Deleuze and Guattari, the key danger, is the profit motive, as well as, not unimportantly, the question of what 'the prospects are for a "person who comes home exhausted, spent after a draining day, who automatically turns on his television" in search of a minor buzz through "another personal reterritorialisation by totally artifical means"' (Guattari in Genosko 2012, 219).

In conclusion, as we possibly shift to what Guattari termed a 'post-media' period, precisely when the internet and digital media have become so ubiquitous, so commonplace as to 'fall to the level of banality of the telephone' (Guattari 2011b, 49), perhaps then our fascination with the media may lessen 'and be replaced by other telematic practices, by interactivity with databases, etc. Media such as the telephone will continue to exist, but it will no longer be invested in the same way' (Guattari 2011b, 49). As Guattari further expands, 'the junction of the audio-visual with telematics and information technology is something that will open up quite incredible possibilities of composition' (2011b, 49), though he stressed that this is by no means a given, which is evidenced by the increased corporatisation of the internet in the last two decades. This is precisely why Deleuze's work is so important. Indeed, Deleuze urges us to 'hijack speech. Creating has always been something different from communicating. The key thing may be to create vacuoles of noncommunication, circuit breakers, so we can elude control' (Deleuze 1995, 175). In this respect their *Anti-Oedipus*, and the meta-model of schizoanalysis they draw out in it (Guattari 1998), is precisely the method to be developed.

CHAPTER FOUR

Play and games

There are numerous links between play and Deleuze and Guattari's understanding of desire. While desire precedes play, as even a mollusc desires reproduction, we find evidence of play in all cultures and in every animal whose actions we can reasonably comprehend. Roger Caillois (Caillois and Barash 2001) argues that our desire to play arises from a desire for a series of sensations, which are all highlighted in Deleuze's work. These 'sensations' include *agon* – the desire to engage with others – inherently linked to making connections and a 'becoming-public of an otherwise private individual' (Buchanan 1997); *alea* – the desire to experience chance – a central element of Deleuze's thinking about the origin of difference and thought (Hughes 2009, 127–32); *mimicry* – the desire to inhabit a different subject position, which relates directly to the notion of becoming (Deleuze and Guattari 1986); as does *illinx* – the desire to experience something unusual and unexpected – which relates to Deleuze's concept of jouissance (Deleuze 2001).

Play, in many senses, is an inherent part of life and an inevitable element of assemblages. Play gives rise to new connections; it accounts for and embraces differences; it offers an opportunity to become something else for a while and remain changed forever as a result. And yet, like desire, play only operates within assemblages – broadly called 'games' – which structure the way play happens and determine what it produces. The goal of this chapter is to give some serious thought to how games and play relate to the work of Deleuze, in the hope of not only showing how we can better understand games but also so we might better understand why we desire to play them.

In his book *Homo Ludens* Huizinga presents an argument that play is an essential part of life and a fundamental component of culture. He argues that play precedes culture and in many senses culture is a 'codification of play' (Huizinga 1948, 46), but that play nevertheless retains the playful ability to challenge and change that particular codification. If we understand that we generally call the establishment of a set of rules to facilitate play a 'game', then, he argues, we can understand society itself as a game (Huizinga 1948, 100–1). The rules of the game are there to help you play and, generally, you need to stick to the rules in order to make sure that the whole game works. There are moments when the game stops producing what it should (fun, enjoyment) and the rules need to be changed. The paradox of the game is that there are necessary rules that provide the freedom to play, but play itself is boundless and creatively challenging to any given set of rules. Play itself allows for different experiences; it allows for an escape from representations (such as rules) and replaces them with creative experiences.

> We have to conclude, therefore, that civilization is, in its earliest phases, played. It does not come *from* play like a baby detaching itself from the womb: it arises *in* and *as* play, and never leaves it. (Huizinga 1948, 173)

This summation of play bears an uncanny resemblance to Deleuze and Guattari's assessment of desire, which they similarly understand to be the intrinsic force behind the development of life as we know it. In Deleuze and Guattari's formulation, it is desire that plays this formative role – the innate drive that ends up giving rise to the machines that create the world as we know it.

> Desire constantly couples continuous flows and partial objects that are by nature fragmentary and fragmented. Desire causes the current to flow, itself flows in turn, and breaks the flows. (Deleuze and Guattari 2004a, 6)

Deleuze and Guattari's understanding of desire and Huizinga's understanding of play share the belief that what has been found is an essential source of energy and motivation that conspires to produce the world we inhabit, or, as Obi Wan describes the Force in *Star Wars*, 'an energy field created by all living things, [that] surrounds us … penetrates us … [and] binds the galaxy together' (Lucas 1977).

Could it possibly be that Huizinga and Deleuze are talking about the same thing? When Deleuze mentions 'desire', is he talking about the playful drive to connect, to experiment and to produce? And when Huizinga mentions 'play', does he mean that play arises from the desire to make these connections? Deleuze notes an 'aleatory' (or luck-based) point that is at the root of all original thought and creation in the universe, a point where the ability to try something different, to become something else, becomes the source of creativity – this is very similar to the properties that Huizinga attributes to play. While there are differences in the relative formulations of desire and play, Deleuze and Huizinga seem to suggest there is a trickster spirit inside of all desire, and what it desires most is to play, to experience different things, and forge new connections, to produce the new. The trickster spirit is kept in check because it knows that without the game there would be less play, without the structures there would be no winners and without respect there would be no one to play with. But maintaining the spirit is a delicate balancing act.

The link between flow and assemblages

William Gibson tells a story that he came up with the idea of 'cyberspace' while watching teenagers play arcade games. He could see that the players were so absorbed by the game space that they had become part of the game and that the players really believed in the space behind the screen.

The kids who were playing them were so physically involved, it seemed to me that what they wanted was to be inside the games, within the notional space of the machine. The real world had disappeared for them, it had completely lost its importance. They were in that notional space, and the machine in front of them was the brave new world. (Gibson and Rosenberg 2014)

In such a description one can see the formation of an assemblage, which is as much composed of the virtual as it is of the actual, which is constituted by a connection between (at least) two otherwise partial objects, united as one through the flow of desire. Gibson was noting the merging of not only reality and virtuality but also the merging of player and machine; they were completely reliant on each other to produce the affect that they did. If you stand back it is clear how the desire of the player and the architecture of the game work together to produce a flow which constitutes one assemblage: visualise the electrons flowing through the machine and flying out of the screen to be received by the player's eyes, generating an electrical flow along synapses in the brain, which fire off neurons and send further electrical flows, which cause muscles to twitch in response, causing fingers to tap and move, again causing electrons to flow through the game processor and produce an effect on the screen; all this happening near instantaneously, creating a reality that is visceral, engaging and immersive – an affective assemblage produced by flow.

Mihaly Csikzentmihalyi suggests that such an experience of 'flow' is integral to experiencing happiness. The state of 'optimal flow' involves meeting a number of criteria:

1 The person must be completely involved in the activity, focused and concentrating.

2 The person will experience a sense of ecstasy, and being outside reality.

3 The person will experience inner clarity. He or she will know what needs to be done and how well he or she is doing.

4 He or she knows the activity is doable, and his or her skills adequate.

5 He or she will experience a sense of serenity, where he or she will be unconcerned about him or herself.

6 He or she will be focused on the present and experience a sense of timelessness.

7 He or she will feel intrinsic motivation. Whatever he or she produces, flow becomes its own reward. (Csikszentmihalyi 2004)

Czikszentmihalyi suggests that it is possible for those with strong and creative minds, who are open to engaging in new and challenging activities, to create their own sense of flow in day-to-day life by controlling their subjective reality and orienting their lives to derive pleasure from their flow production (Csikszentmihalyi 1990). He describes this ability as belonging to an *autotelic* personality – someone able to set his or her own goals and manufacture his or her own flow (Csikszentmihalyi 1990, 67). However, it is also clear that such flow can be enabled through connections with very well-designed machines (Black et al. 2008, 12). For *homo ludens*, games are those things that can create and sustain flow. The rules of a game are designed to allow players to experience flow. The better the game is, the more absorbed you become in it. The more it is suited to your particular level of skill and interest, the more you lose yourself in the process. You do it because you enjoy it, not simply because of what it produces, but, of course, games do produce things and they produce them very efficiently at that.

Both our play and our desire are in some sense controlled and maintained by the codifications that end up channelling the energy invested in the assemblage. We identify games as assemblages that manage to harness and channel the feeling of play, and produce joy, amongst other things. We understand that the structure of the game is in some sense the thing that gives rise to the affect because it is the game that gives us the element to focus on, that assembles the pieces of the universe into a coherent meaning and that gives us a role to *play*. In all, the game channels our playful desire in a way that allows our desire to flow, manages to sustain our desire and also makes our desire productive. As Huizinga understands it, this means that society is, in some sense, a game.

Of course the engagement provided by flow is also, in some sense, distracting, absorbing, stupifying. Raymond Williams talks about flow in the sense of capture, arguing that we are absorbed by the flow of information on our television sets because we are so engaged and, subsequently, pacified (Williams 2003, 94–5). This pacifying property of flow can be explained in terms of fluid dynamics, and specifically Bernoulli's principle that states 'where the speed of the flow increases, the pressure and potential energy decreases'. This physical principle is what makes a plane's wing generate lift as it moves through the air. The air travels further over the curved surface on top of the wing than it does on the straight line on the bottom; thus the air moves faster above the wing and creates a low pressure, which the high pressure beneath the wing moves toward, lifting the wing in the process. The same principle applies with games and flow: when flow is taking place, we experience a lack of pressure; when it slows, or stops, pressure builds up. As a game or system designer one way you can avoid pressure building is to maintain the flow. The same thing applies to machines and desires. It is when desire does not flow that the problems arise: flow in many senses keeps everything running smoothly and undermines the development of pressure, leakages and ruptures.

To return briefly to the extended analogy between the flow of desire and the flow of play, if we can see how Huizinga interprets 'society' as a game-like codification of the play spirit, it is worth pointing out that Deleuze and Guattari understand capitalism as a codification of desire. Capitalism is the greatest game of all and it functions all the more smoothly because it is able to generate connections, maintain the flow of desire, keep desire productive, all the while ensuring that the flows are maintained so that there is no point of pressure or resistance in the system. The remainder of this chapter will focus on how Deleuze and Guattari's concepts can be used to analyse the flow of play in games, but it is worth remembering that the same concepts can be applied to the flow of desire in society.

The smooth and the striated

Deleuze and Guattari themselves argue that one of the key elements of analysing games is to understand the game space as a combination of smooth and striated spaces (Deleuze and Guattari 2004b, 551). A quick summary of the role of the smooth and striated in Deleuze and Guattari's work shows that they attribute all manner of characteristics to each type of space. Throughout their work the smooth is composed of differences; it is open and free of limitations; it is composed by the movement of particles, which are able to move freely within it. One distributes oneself within a smooth space and inhabits it as one wishes, such as nomads moving across a landscape, smoothing it out as they go. On the other hand, striated spaces are dominated by lines, directions, enclosures that close off certain parts of the terrain according to a central and overarching 'goal'. Striated space tends to be homogeneous and controlled, whereas the smooth is constituted by difference and disjuncture

(Deleuze and Guattari 2004b, 530–9). There are numerous other 'echoes' of this difference between the smooth and striated in Deleuze and Guattari's work: the striations of arborescent structures are compared to the heterogeneous smoothness of rhizomes; the dominant, imperial major literature is compared to the responsive and itinerant minor literature; and, perhaps most fundamentally, difference is compared to repetition.

Striated game spaces are those filled with lines – they work by delineating specific rules that enable a sort of 'coming together' of playfulness, so that the desire to be playful can be engaged and sustained. When two puppies are playing they will give each other 'playful nips', a light bite that is not a bite but also that is not *not* a bite (Sutton-Smith 2006, 297). The line that delineates the playful nip from the bite is the line that makes the play a part of a game. As long as the puppies follow the rules, then the game can continue, but should one of them 'cross the line' and bite too hard, then the game ends and the play stops. Make no mistake, the playfulness can take place without the rules, but – through either design, repetition or trial and error – it is made apparent that sticking to the rules ensures that the play can continue for longer, and thus a striation appears. This line between 'game' space and non-game space has been described by ludologists as 'the magic circle', a delineated space where participants agree to play by certain rules in the interest of sustaining their enjoyment (Woods 2009, 205). So here is the first rule of game design: the game space must involve striations; it must invoke rules that delineate what can and cannot be done, in order to maintain the flow of play among the players. It is a space that must create lines.

The example of the 'playful nip' also serves to illustrate the smooth space in games – a space that allows for and encourages experimentation and experiences that are not strictly determined by reality, yet are not *not* real, in the sense that they still produce effects. In this sense, all games set up a virtual field of action, and their rules (or their program in digital games) are designed to immerse you in that field and accept its reality. Deleuze and Guattari have a sophisticated understanding of the virtual, which rests upon the notion that the virtual is always already a part of the real, rather than opposed to it (Ansell-Pearson 2005). Instead of understanding the virtual as a pure abstraction that exists as separate to, and in many ways opposed to, the real, the virtual can be understood as defining the fields of possibilities for the real to inhabit generating experiences and effects in the process. The playful nip is an actual instance of a virtual bite, absolutely real at all points, but not what it 'actually' is. Following this logic, game machines set up a virtual field of experiences that may not be materially determined but nevertheless relate directly to the real. When game players agree that an avatar will 'represent' them in a game space, they realise that they are not the avatar – nevertheless, they will understand the actions and experiences of the avatar as specifically 'not *not* real'. Through this engagement with the virtual, a good game will elicit all sorts of effects upon the player. Playing games with smooth spaces allows for an experience of what Deleuze and Guattari call *a becoming* – an increased awareness of what it is to be something other than oneself. The well-designed game opens up a field of action and makes the effect of those actions real and immanent enough to generate an effect upon the player, so the player is 'drawn in' by the tangibility of the experience of the virtual to the extent that it generates an effect upon the real. If you are playing a game of *Monopoly* and experience a thrill of power and control when someone lands on your Mayfair hotel, then you are experiencing a moment of becoming-millionaire property tycoon. If you are playing *Alien Isolation* and feel your heart rate and blood pressure surge as you hear Geiger's nightmarish alien slowly approach your hiding place, you are experiencing a becoming-hunted, becoming-Amanda Ripley. The virtuality of these experiences does not negate the reality of their effects, and the better a game is the more it encourages a true experience of what it is like to be something other than yourself, caught up in the imperatives of your actual machines. This is not to say the experience provided through playing games is in some sense intractable – the point is that what emerges from the virtual is a mix between what is possible and what is achievable given your material constraints. Your experience of 'becoming-millionaire tycoon' might be thoroughly impeded by your co-players' insistence on continually stealing from the bank, undermining the coherence of the game, but at the same time still allowing you a particular form of becoming. The emergence of the properties of the game, any game, is a product of both the game and the players: 'meaning and doing transpire in the same gamic gesture' (Galloway 2006, 104). So the second attribute of any good game design must create smooth spaces that encourage and facilitate becoming-other. It needs to lift you away from the world you are in and allow you to experience it differently in the process of experiencing another world altogether.

Deleuze and Guattari suggest that the analysis of games ought to proceed through an examination of the game space; we imagine they mean paying attention to the striated spaces that allow play to flow by creating a sense of process, and the smooth spaces that facilitate becoming, innovation and creativity. Deleuze and Guattari provide the ancient Chinese game of *Go* as an example of a game of smooth space and *Chess* as a game of striated space (Deleuze and Guattari 2004b, 551). *Go*, despite its heavily striated board space, is defined by its relatively basic set of rules and incredibly complicated and emergent game play. Aside from the two basic rules, the way *Go* plays really depends upon the players, and there is an adage that no two games of *Go* are ever the same. On the other hand, Deleuze and Guattari present *Chess* as an example of a striated game space. *Chess* has a large number of quite sophisticated rules, which define quite specific possibilities within the game. This has given rise to particular tactics and manoeuvres that have become 'transcendental' in the sense that series of moves such as the 'Ruy Lopez' and the 'Sicilian Defence' are well known and used repeatedly. These standardised approaches have developed thanks to the far more limited options available to the player.

It would be tempting from this summary to suggest that smooth spaces are important for creating play and striated spaces are important for sustaining play, but both spaces are implicated in constructing an assemblage that channels flows of play. It is the striations that establish the 'rules of the game' and the smooth spaces that allow for 'playfulness' and it is important that all games combine the two sorts of spaces to ensure that play flows. One way to illustrate this is to compare the first-person shooters *Fallout 3* and *Bioshock Infinite*. The latter, despite its name, hides a relatively formulaic game engine (striated space) behind an incredibly rich and interesting narrative (smooth space). The storyline and 'background' of *Bioshock Infinite* provides you with the experience of becoming other, highlighting the tenuous nature of both agency and determinacy and the possibility of being-multiple and pursuing fractal pathways. However, the game play itself is incredibly linear, requiring you to move along an established pathway without variation, fulfilling the same goals as every other player before you, and achieving the same outcome. *Fallout 3*, provides an open game play space that you can move through according to your own interests, and it features game objectives that change according to the decisions you make. However, the story itself is far more 'linear' in the sense that your simple goal is to find out what happened to your father, even though the way you pursue that goal, and indeed whether you pursue it at all, is entirely up to you. Both games are excellent examples of the genre and each works because their striated spaces – the linearity of gameplay in *Bioshock* and the linearity of the central narrative in *Fallout* – are easily overcome by the open spaces provided by the imaginative narrative and the open, contingent world respectively.

The point is that while it is possible to assess the smooth spaces of games according to whether they encourage becomings, and the striated spaces according to whether they effectively channel flow, the most interesting aspect of game design is how the striated gives rise to the smooth, and vice versa (Deleuze and Guattari 2004b, 551). In an interview where he discusses the game of tennis, Deleuze describes his fascination with how play styles have evolved and how the game of tennis has changed as different players have attempted new and novel techniques and approaches to the game. He identifies Bjorn Borg as an innovator, playing the back of the court with powerful strokes hit high over the net; his style was in opposition to the serve/volley orthodoxy and thus created a smooth space above a previous striation. Of course, when he began to win everything, all players began to copy Borg, meaning that playing tennis again became striated until the next innovator arrived to redraw the lines.

> the history of sport runs through these inventors, each of whom amounts to something unforeseen, a new syntax, a transformation, and without them the purely technological advances would have remained quantitative, irrelevant, and pointless. (Deleuze 1995, 132)

The three syntheses of
desiring-playful-production

Here Deleuze and Guattari seem to suggest that another way to assess or analyse games is to assess how they engage our desire to create something new. If *agon*, *alea*, *mimicry* and *illinx* are employed to motivate our desire to play, does that necessarily mean that you are playing a 'good game', or are you being tricked into a flow that simply reproduces repression? History is replete with examples of play being used to 'dupe' the masses, as a tool to maintain the flow and keep the pressure low as a result. Businesses use game-like competition between workers and management to increase production and the aleatory thrill of playing lotteries and gambling has long been understood as a way to get money out of the poor and the desperate. The games we play are also, inevitably, productive, so another way to assess the quality of a game is to consider what the game produces.

Deleuze and Guattari argue that flow produces different things through the 'three processes of desiring-production'. While Deleuze and Guattari are explicitly talking about the flows of desire, we are reading desire and play as essentially the same thing – an innate drive that both shapes and reconfigures the world as we find it; as it flows, so does it shape the world through its connections, recordings and consumptions. Deleuze and Guattari begin their exploration of capitalism and schizophrenia with an examination of how desire is productive (Deleuze and Guattari 2004b, 1–54). In doing this they identify three particular processes of production as 'syntheses' (synthesis referring to the joining, reconciliation or embedding of flows). The first of these is the connective synthesis – it is the moment of encounter and it produces an engagement which facilitates a flow. In gaming it is the participation in the game, the joining of the player to the game like a mouth to a nipple. It is the production of production – the feeling that 'this is fun, let's keep doing it'. The second synthesis is the disjunctive synthesis, which is the production of recording, the attempt to reconcile play with past and future experiences, to ascribe to it a set of rules. This attempt is always in some sense doomed to fail, but the attempt is the thing that produces game rules through repetition and difference. The third synthesis is the conjunctive synthesis, which allows play/desire to once again become productive by allowing the flow to engage with other machines. It is again the production of production, but this time the flow produced is not brought back into the game machine but rather is connected to and consumed by another – it is the production of consumption. So put in more simple terms, any time we play, we produce three things: we produce a connection that creates a flow, we produce a recording that 'remembers' the flow and we produce a flow that can be plugged into other machines to become productive.

According to Deleuze and Guattari, each of these syntheses has a legitimate and illegitimate use, and we can use these designations to determine whether what a game produces is positive or whether it actually produces repression.[1] The legitimate use of the connective synthesis is inclusive, partial and non-specific, meaning that the connections made by a game are easy to engage with, iterative, not predetermined and easily changeable. On the other hand, the illegitimate use of the connective synthesis is exclusive, global and specific: that is, the game is somewhat closed off, exclusive and the manner of connections to be made is pre-defined, inflexible and exactly the same for everyone. This tension between the quality of connections made by games has often been evident in arguments about the relative benefits of social games such as board games, or team games versus solo games, such as single-player quest games (Woods 2007). The argument is that the social game gives rise to a far more inclusive, partial and non-specific series of connections, while video games tend toward the exclusive, global and specific mode. While playing a social game, the game itself establishes a framework for interaction, but it does not define that interaction. The kinds of connections that can be made in the game are up to the player and the enjoyment comes from the emergent properties of the game space as a result (Willson 2015). Compare this to the linearity of most solo-player games, such as *Bioshock Infinite*, and it's clear that while the player does do some of the work of determining how the game will 'feel', or how it might progress, for the most part these attributes of the game are already determined. The kind of connections the game can produce (at least in game) are somewhat exclusive – already determined and inflexible. Should you wish to start a conversation with a non-playing character, for instance, you can only do so if the NPC is programmed to do so.

The illegitimate and legitimate uses of the second synthesis (the production of recording) are best understood by examining the way game rules are developed and implemented. Deleuze and Guattari refer to the legitimate use of the second synthesis as being both free and reactive, as opposed to the illegitimate use, which takes the transcendental and immovable as ideal. Since the second synthesis produces a 'recording', we might be best served by thinking of good games that develop their own rules, or play that becomes reactive to local conditions, instead of simply staying the same. Playing with children often illustrates the problems with clinging too hard and fast to 'the rules', as children become bored and 'sick of this game' when their spirit of adventure yearns for a new kind of stimulus. The same ambivalence can be shown in the board game community towards 'rules lawyering', where adherence to the rules is pursued well beyond the point where any joy has long been extinguished. The problem of 'recording' eliminating difference is particularly evident in video games, where repetitive plays of the game tend to produce identical experiences. On the *Donkey Kong* 'game and watch', a hand-held game from the 1980s, *Donkey Kong* would throw his barrels at Mario in one of two or three pre-programmed patterns. Once you knew which pattern was being pursued, you could complete the first screen by simply pressing the buttons in a repetitive way, in full confidence that Donkey Kong would do nothing else but what he'd been pre-programmed to do. Such an adherence to the 'rules' meant that the joy of playing the game was not really engaged until you progressed past the first few challenges and the permutations of Donkey Kong's and Mario's possible actions became too complex to anticipate.

Of course, game designers are aware of this issue, and have produced ever more sophisticated 'artificial intelligences' to ensure that the game experience remains rich and varied, even for repeat players. The aforementioned *Alien Isolation* includes an alien antagonist that will change its behaviour based upon what the player does. For instance, the first time a player throws a flash grenade down a corridor, the alien will be distracted and go to investigate (giving the player a chance to escape). However, the second or third time the player uses this technique, the alien will see behind the ruse, and will instead seek out the player who is creating the distractions. In this way the game presents a challenge for the player who is forced to come up with new strategies and tactics in order to succeed, and has a far more immersive and affective experience as a result.

> 'Something we learned very early on is we couldn't make an enemy that was scripted,' said lead gameplay designer Gary Napper. 'We needed something that would be different every time you played it. You're going to die a lot, which means restarting a lot, and if the alien was scripted, you'd see the same behaviour. That makes the alien become predictable, and a lot less scary.' (Batchelor 2014)

Through 'changing the patterns and the rules', a good game creates a space where the possible paths to experience, enjoy and succeed in the game become multiple and remain reactive to the player's actions and desires. In the legitimate second synthesis of recording, the local takes precedence over the transcendental and produces an awareness of difference.

The third and final synthesis of production is the production of consumption. This accounts for the way flows of play feed into other machines and produce affects. The legitimate use of this synthesis is one that channels energy into a local and contingent affect. The illegitimate use tends towards a 'segregative and mobbing' affect.

> What the two uses of the conjunctive synthesis amount to then is different ways of investing in the social, both operating at the level of the unconscious, not the conscious ... the [illegitimate] mode invests desire in conformance of the interests of a dominant class, but operates on its own account; the mode Deleuze and Guattari consider [legitimate] invests in desire in what they call a transversal manner, which means it operates in such a way as to cut across barriers of race, class and gender. It sets in motion new types of flows that the old, established break-flows (Oedipus in league with the family and the State) cannot handle ... (Buchanan 2000, 27)

Games often operate to invest desire in the 'interests of the dominant class'. The use of the game *America's Army* as a recruitment tool for the US armed forces is the paradigmatic example of how the experience of play can be reinvested in becoming productive for the institutions of the establishment (Cremin 2016, 132; Lenderman 2006, 222). However, the use of games to recreate control is also evident in the competitiveness used to drive productivity increases throughout workplaces, and games are also increasingly used to spread marketing messages, feeding the exhilaration of immersion straight back into the machines of capitalism.[2] Some game/player assemblages fail to connect their flows to anything outside themselves, reinvesting their flows only within the game, and their flows remain 'captured' as a result (Cook 2009). Similarly, the use of play to generate compulsive consumption and aggregate marketing data, such as evident in many 'fremium' social games and immersive marketing games, is far more likely to extend the chances of capturing desire than it is likely to produce moments of emancipatory becoming (Leaver and Willson 2015). Such investments of the desire to play are inherently reactionary, prescribed by power to make play (and desire) produce its own repression.

Alternatively, the legitimate use of the conjunctive synthesis can be understood to facilitate the coming together of difference under the field of play. This investment of the play spirit ensures that the game generates an awareness of the difference among its players. It manages to create an engagement that is capable of transcending social and material boundaries and manufactures multiple kinds of becoming-other: for instance, an international soccer match that brings together two otherwise alienated cultures and forces a playful engagement with their differences; or an alternative reality game that produces a community that is then able to use its collective problem-solving abilities to tackle larger world problems.[3] The process of play done well engages the 'player as artist' (Cremin 2012, 73). The game forms an assemblage that connects the player with the play community through 'creative processual activity' that encourages a becoming-public and becoming-other that allows for new experiences and assemblages to emerge (Colman 2012, 262).

To summarise, then, when judging the games we play, it is worth remembering that the desire to play can be assessed in terms of what it produces. While it is always possible to smooth over striations and then draw new lines upon smooth spaces while playing, we can determine the value of the game by examining what it produces at each stage of the three syntheses of production: the production of connection, the production of recording and the production of consumption. A paradigmatic example of the illegitimate production within the gaming community can be seen in the gamergate movement. Gamergate is a protest movement that has emerged in active resistance to the inclusion of females in the gaming community. The movement specifically criticises 'Social Justice Warriors' that campaign against the exclusion and misogynistic portrayal of women in games. Members of the gamergate movement have actively threatened gamers who have critiqued misogyny in games and/or have developed games that challenge the hyper-masculine gaming hegemony (Tomkinson and Harper 2015, 617–18). The gamergate movement can be seen to be a product of the illegitimate investment of the desire to play at all three syntheses. In the first instance, the gamergate movement arises from an exclusive community of 'basement dwelling manboys' (Sheffield 2013), which has been formed through the exclusive connections of the broader game marketing machine. The marketing machine created the category of 'boy games' by preconceiving their consumers as socially isolated, disempowered, sex-starved loners and by creating games that represent the hypermasculine fantasies of violence, power and their binary opposite of servile, hyper-feminised women. In the illegitimate use of the second fantasy, these tropes of women-as-victim, women-as-other are repeated ad nauseam, without alteration, without challenge and, significantly, without any flexibility in game to negotiate or change the allocated gender roles. In the third and final synthesis of consumption, the strongly delineated, patriarchal play experience imprints itself on the gaming community, such that the gamergaters start to identify the source of their own repression (games for boys!) and defend its exclusiveness and infallibility, to the benefit of game designers who can produce the same old misogynistic rubbish knowing they'll maintain their flows of consumption. The isolated gamergaters caught in this trap fight for their own repression as stubbornly as though it was their salvation.

On the other hand, the desire to play can be harnessed by the legitimate uses of the three syntheses of production in order to produce a fundamentally better world. Ludologists such as Jane McGonigal (McGonigal 2011) and Edward Castranova (Castronova 2007) have written extensively about examples of games building communities and creative capacity. Games work by creating processual activities of engagement; they generate flows of desire, bring to light the unique talent of each participant and allow those talents to build a collective and creative capacity, all the while maintaining the sense of enjoyment and 'flow'. Perhaps the best way to summarise the positive elements of play and games is to quote one of the targets of the gamergate movement, game-celebrity Felicia Day: 'Games are beautiful, they are creative, they are worlds to immerse yourself in. They are art. And they are worth fighting for' (Day 2014). Or, as Guattari notes:

> The machinic production of subjectivity can work for the better or for the worse. At best there is the creation, or invention, of new Universes of reference, at worst there is the deadening influence of the mass media to which millions are currently condemned. (Guattari 1995, 5)

Play and desire offer so much potential for creating worlds of experimentation, camaraderie and joy. The question then becomes why do we continue playing the same old games when we could simply change the rules?

CHAPTER FIVE

News and information media

Information is only the strict minimum necessary for the emission, transmission, and observation of orders as commands.

(DELEUZE AND GUATTARI 2004b, 84)

Watching the news is like plugging back into your family. You listen attentively to father as he tells you how the world really is while mother issues kind words of assurance and you are rendered dumb and mute, lacking the knowledge they have and the ability to contribute to the discussion. Some would have it that this is normal, that news is about replacing our lack of information – filling a void; on the other hand there is the conviction that it doesn't have to be like this, that maybe what we're being told is part of a regime of oppression. Rather than extending our potential actions, maybe news media seek to divert those energies and maintain the status quo. This chapter examines how 'News' has evolved and seeks to discover what it is that news really produces.

What is the news for?

When we think about the purpose of news it becomes apparent that the news is an assemblage that operates for a number of different purposes. We currently find ourselves absolutely surrounded by different media that serve the purpose of relaying 'the news'. The qualities of what constitutes news has also undergone a series of changes as a result. Broadcast news remains steadfastly oedipal in its presentation of daddy (holder of power and information), mummy (worldly and comforting) and you, the consumer, necessarily lacking in knowledge, insight and interaction, beholden to and subconsciously enamoured with your *pappamama*. However, that traditional news machine is increasingly under assault from a more rhizomatic and engaging system of news feeds, citizen journalism and click-throughs. Understanding the future of news requires an initial understanding of the desires that give rise to the product of 'news'.

The common argument is that the 'news machine' has developed as an extension of the desire to share information. We can understand sharing news as an inherent attempt to connect with one another. As a thought experiment, consider the first instance of communication between two humans. It may well be that the first thing that one human ever 'said' to another human may have been an aggressive roar before some kind of conflict. In this instance, the desire to communicate arises from the desire to intimidate, but it is still a desire to share information. However, it is equally possible that the first instance of human communication happened when one person sought to make an intimate connection with another. At this point, there is an inherent attempt to understand one another. As Aristotle noted many years ago, humanity distinguishes itself through its elaborate languages for sharing news (Aristotle 1999). Deleuze takes this claim somewhat further by establishing that what really distinguishes human communication is the ability to use languages made up of 'hearsay, or reported speech' (Deleuze and Guattari 1987, 84). As Buchanan has pointed out, bees and dogs may communicate things to each other directly, through dancing and barking respectively, but only humans have the ability to relate what has happened to someone else through the use of a language (Buchanan 2000, 108–9). The basic difference between the language of bees and the language of humans is that human language draws on concepts that refer to things outside the direct experience of the speaker.

Deleuze argues that any attempt to communicate involves the production of concepts (Buchanan 2000, 60–2), little machines or 'collective assemblages', that enable the process of understandable communication (or 'enunciation') (Deleuze and Guattari

1987, 88). However, while humans tend to collaboratively create concepts in conjunction with their lived experience, the operation of news, particularly in the mode of 'mass media', tends to impose concepts upon us. What we see in communication is the development of 'established codes', which act as a sort of shorthand of understanding. This is prevalent in all news where stories are consistently 'framed' in order to render a story understandable in a certain way. Information itself is inherently ambiguous and any information 'is characterised by a multiplicity of possible interpretations and perspectives' (Iyengar 1990, 20). News operates to simplify the world for us, to make it understandable and provide us with the sense that the world *is* sensible.

> Newspapers, news, proceed by redundancy, in that they tell us what we 'must' think, retain, expect etc. Language is neither informational nor communicational. It is not the communication of information but something quite different: the transmission of order words, either from one statement to another or within each statement, insofar as each statement accomplishes an act and the act is accomplished in the statement. (Deleuze and Guattari 1987, 87)

If, then, we can understand news as such an assemblage that brings order to the world by rendering events understandable in a particular way, what then is the organising principle of that assemblage? What does the news desire? What kind of order does it produce? How does the process of news making mediate the flow of desire? And what kind of order is produced in this process? In order to answer these questions, we should turn to the Deleuzean concept of the Body without Organs (BwO).

What is a body without organs?

Defining a BwO is not something that is done easily. Nevertheless, when we think about the evolution of news it becomes clear that the 'organising principle' of news plays an important role in determining how news evolved. The notion of an 'organising principle' relates directly to what Deleuze and Guattari call a body without organs, or, as we discussed in the context of faciality, an abstract machine. Consider what a BwO might be by thinking first of what a body *with* organs is: that is, it is a machine made up of machines. It is at all points a composite of the various desiring machines that go into it. At any point it is a compilation of 'eating machines, speaking machines, shitting and fucking machines' (Deleuze and Guattari 2004a, 1); each of these machines feeds upon flows of desire – the desire for, or perhaps rather, the desire that is connection, the desire that is production, the desire that is reproduction. Deleuze and Guattari are at pains to point out that the world we encounter is in many ways produced by the way these machines process desire. However, the notion of the body 'without organs' complicates the effect of these machines by raising the question of how desire might be controlled or channelled by more abstract forces. Deleuze and Guattari took the term 'body without organs' from Antonin Artaud's radio play *To Have Done With the Judgment of God*, which features the lines:

> When you will have made him a body without organs,
> then you will have delivered him from all his automatic reactions
> and restored him to his true freedom. (Artaud 1976, 571)

Artaud seems to be speaking of allowing desire to escape the confines of his machines – to have a purpose beyond 'automatic reaction'.[1] In this sense we can understand one of the uses of the BwO is to think beyond what the machine does, to start thinking about why it does so – what principle are the flows of desire organised around? Another philosopher might use the term 'ideal' here to describe an abstract idea that reality conforms to – more or less.[2] However, Deleuze and Guattari reject the notion of ideals: such notions are power-laden attempts to reduce difference. But the concept of the BwO can't do that because the body, even when thinking beyond the need of any particular organs, is still in every way both a machine and product made of organs – what the body is possible of doing is in some sense limited by its machines – but it is not limited to only what each machine can do. The BwO is a way of thinking of how a particular collective assemblage of particular machines (organs) can go on to produce something that is greater than what each particular organ could produce on its own. The notion of a 'body' as an emergent collective of machines provides an 'organising principle' for what that collective could possibly do. In understanding the 'organising principle' we can open up our understanding of the possibilities contained within assemblages, while remaining aware that what is produced is still a function of the assemblage. Hence the BwO can be helpfully understood as another term for of an 'abstract machine'; it is a concept that Deleuze and Guattari use to define the organising principle and, resultantly, the conditioned possibilities of machines.

One way of understanding the role of the BwO in relation to media machines is to think about the conflicting purposes of news. In the case of news, there is a pertinent dilemma about whether the organising principle of news is either to inform or to entertain. The differences between these 'organising principles' condition how the news assemblage is structured and, in turn, changes the product of that machine.

The history of the news assemblage

Let us take a step back from Deleuze, Guattari and their BwO to consider the history of how the 'news machine' has developed. To do this, we'll turn to Jürgen Habermas's account of the development of journalism in his book *The Structural Transformation of the Public Sphere* (Habermas 1989). Discussing the development of the commercial media, Habermas traces the development of a literate reading public to the rise of 'salons and coffee houses' in eighteenth-century Europe. These public spaces would become known as places to receive information from distant lands. But of course, the rise of bars, clubs and salons only represented a *relatively* secular and inclusive 'institutionalisation' of a practice of information sharing that has forever provided the basis of the 'community' assemblage. Community spaces have always been used to channel flows of information: the church used its control of that flow to institutionalise its power; town criers provided a one-way flow of information from the feudal rulers. Village greens and pubs provided a much more local and immanent flow, but, until the invention of the printing press, the flow of that information was limited by the amount of human movement between communities, and the flow of stories. Nevertheless, these flows of information were still fundamental to determining what the community assemblage looked like and what it produced. Social and architectural structures were arranged to maximise the amount of order (and/or flow) that could be generated by information.

The oral and embodied nature of information allowed for very easy control of how that information was transferred: by literally controlling stories and bodies, one could control the flow. This gave profound power to those who due to architectural or institutional power were able to tell the same stories consistently, the power of the church and feudal lords being emblematic. However, as touched on in the chapter on assemblages, with the invention of the printing press the assemblage of information flow radically changed and, with it, so did the social and architectural structures it produced. Perhaps the most obvious challenge to the previous oral, institutional and corporeal power could be seen in Martin Luther's publication of his ninety-five theses, which challenged the legitimacy of the papal system. These words were able to spread as far as one could carry a book and could be spread in many directions at the same time, facilitated by mechanical mass production of print. Mechanised printing presented a new distribution machine.[3] Once printed, the words did not require an institution to defend them or repeat them. No matter how many hands his arguments passed through, the words stayed the same, retaining their revolutionary zeal. No longer could the simple control of bodies translate into the control of information. Such writing spread on the back of the growing mercantile class in Europe; as more and more trade took place between distant lands, more and more information flowed with that trade. The development of the news machine thereby coincided with the opening up of a whole range of flows: flows of goods for trade, flows of money for investment and eventually flows of ideas about life, religion and governance. The opening up of these flows affected a whole series of other machines, undermining the authority of the church and the divine right of kings. The increase in flow of goods and people, along with the increased connection this generated with surrounding areas, undermined the possibility of controlling information by controlling bodies, while the increasing economic benefits of flow ushered in the slow decline of the walled city and the move from city states to nation states, and from the rule of kings to a democracy of the wealthy and powerful.

Of course, information was among the most valuable of the commodity flows that supported the growth of a new economic elite, and this lucrative flow of information created a news machine all of itself. Habermas argues that once it became clear that there was profit to be made from opening up flows of information, businesses such as the publishers of journals, pamphleteers, coffee shops and salons all started making the *quality* of their news their organising principle – their BwO. While their ideal was 'quality' news, the news that was produced was still largely determined by the machines and flows they had available. In the first instance, those who profited were the spaces that prospered out of being the location of news publications. Public houses (pubs), coffee shops and salons created comfortable spaces where people would come together to share information. These small houses became machines of their own, combining flows of locals and travellers with flows of food and drink. The development of the printing press amplified the virtual component of the machine. Now, news didn't just rely on the movement, memory and articulation of a particular traveller, but rather could contain a digest of massive amounts of information pertaining to areas of very specific interest. From these public houses, a new form of public discussion emerged – the exchange of news and views through journals and journalism.

Salons and coffee shops were willing to pay a premium to gather the best information. Given the physicality of the journals themselves, and the costs of distributing them, reading them involved actually going to the salon. Salon owners thus considered that having the information would mean wealthy clientele would want to spend time and money in their salon. Such a centralised mode of information distribution had the unintended benefit of bringing people together to discuss 'what's new'.[4] The mixture of local, lived experience with news from far away created a proliferation of connections, opening up all kinds of intersecting flows and, Habermas argues, created a habit of public communication that marked the zenith of public discussion. According to him, this combination of flows of wealth and information sparked the democratic revolutions of the eighteenth and nineteenth centuries.

Habermas describes this period of history as a high point of democratic engagement, as the state was directly influenced by the learned discussion of the bourgeoisie and the news played its role in reordering a more just and equal society (Habermas 1989,

89–129). However, Deleuze and Guattari describe the same period as one of 'despotism', where the state sought to assert its legitimacy through establishing nationalism, state welfare and representative democracy, all of which serve to capture otherwise revolutionary flows of desire (Deleuze and Guattari 2004a, 237–9). Nationalism institutionalises the notion of community within the state, welfare institutionalises social care within the state and representative democracy institutionalises the expression of power within the state. The role of the news, according to Deleuze's formulation, is to ensure that these desires are channelled towards the preservation of the state, where otherwise they would work towards its abolition. While Habermas lauds the democratic revolutions because they gave the state a semblance of legitimacy, Deleuze sees that the appearance of such legitimacy is a moment of crisis and capture for the flow of desire.

However, both Habermas and Deleuze agree that the state (whether despotic or legitimate) was quickly overtaken by the forces of capitalism as the ordering principle for information. In the process of forging connections and opening up flows, the news machine started interacting with other machines. Perhaps most importantly, the machines of news distribution provided the perfect foil for those capitalists who sought to increase exposure for their commercial products and services – the flow of news is not just about making connections and producing habits, but also about producing consumption. If you were selling London's finest horse whips, how better to advertise your product than by letting people know about it in the journal read by London's wealthiest horse owners? The intersection of the flow of information with the flow of selling products had a number of enduring effects on the flow of news. In the first instance, business people were happy to pay journals to carry pieces that advertised the qualities of their products. This flow of capital became more and more important to newspapers up until the point where advertising revenue became a far larger contributor to the news business than the sales revenues (Habermas 1989, 184). The advent of the penny press in the mid-nineteenth century is probably the clearest indication that, at this point, the value of the newspaper business had moved away from providing flows of valuable information to providing flows of valuable advertising; instead of disseminating information that would prove most valuable to its readers, the organising principle of news was now to produce information that would bring the largest possible audience to advertisers.

The increased flow of advertising capital had a number of other effects on the news machine. With the emphasis placed on securing audiences for advertisers, local news became more and more viable; similarly, the benefit of having information-rich news was soon outweighed by the benefit of having universally appealing news. The largest readerships could guarantee the highest prices for advertising space, hence the object of news making became to channel content towards popular consumption, rather than to generate content that would be valuable for its information. This is not to say that news stopped having valuable informational content, or that it didn't always have the interests of commerce at heart. What we are hoping to point out is that, following the shift from sales to advertising as the major source of revenue, the organising principle of news shifted and thereby changed the way the assemblage operated.

Revisiting the BwO: News is what someone doesn't want you to print

This is where an understanding of the concept of BwO can become inherently valuable to understanding the role of news. In the above analysis of the development of the news assemblage, what is missing is a strong notion of the difference between 'flows of information' and 'flows of advertising'. Is not advertising, in some sense, valuable information? Advertisers generally say so. Similarly, if *all* communication is a procession of order words, isn't all news a form of advertising? The answer for Deleuze is essentially yes: if we understand the news machine as an expression of the machines that go into making up the flow of news, then information and advertising are essentially the same thing. However, it is clear that there *is* a difference between information that is empirical, factual and in the public interest (news) and information that is subjective, figurative and pursuing private interests (advertising). The difference in many respects lies in the ability of the machine to generate and determine its own flows in resistance to administrative and economic power. 'News', as the adage goes, 'is what somebody doesn't want you to print. Everything else is advertising'.

While it is clear how information as advertising is productive, it is not eminently obvious how information as antagonism to power is productive. The orientation towards printing things that people don't want printed can only be maintained if one ignores the immediate commercial need of the news machine, and maintains a commitment towards the principle of sharing information – that is, by building a BwO that maintains an orientation towards sharing information in the face of the machines that otherwise control the flow of information.

Urstaat news

The news does not automatically conform to the organising principle of sharing unwanted information. On the contrary, the flow of news is certainly greatest when the information is superimposed upon other forms of flow. The machinations of celebrities, the diffusion of dominant social myths and, most significantly, the interests of advertisers and newspaper owners are profoundly over-represented in most news industries. All that state news cares about is maintaining the flows. 'Urstaat' is Deleuze and Guattari's term for the 'state-as-concept', which can also be understood as the recurrence of the idea that a centralising and stabilising organisation (such as the state) is an inherently good thing. According to Deleuze, the state-as-concept has undergone a few epochal transformations, from the control of connections and meanings in the savage state to the control over rules and movements in the despotic state (nation state) to the control over flows and money in the current capitalist stage (Deleuze and Guattari 2004b, 284). In every instance, the role of the state has been to regulate the flows – flows of culture in the first instance, flows of people and goods in the second, flows of desire and money in the third. The command of the flow is what allows the urstaat to retain its power. That is why we call 'mass media' news 'urstaat news', because even though it is oriented toward making money, it has an inherent tendency to ensure nothing much changes and everything stays the same.[5]

This progression of how control is maintained can be seen in the current goals of urstaat media – they are no longer there to sell state ideology, or even to support the state in the first instance; they are there to generate flows of money. Mass media magnates have often stated that they don't care about the editorial policies of their newspapers as long as they sell (Evans, 1984; Randall, 2006). For Deleuze and Guattari this is an expression of the capitalist axiomatic – nothing really matters as long as the money keeps flowing – but the flows themselves, as expressions of the machines that channel them, are always oriented toward maintaining stability, maintaining the status quo.

Within media studies, Herman and Chomsky's 'Propaganda Model' of journalistic production is the traditional lens through which state and commercial control over news is assessed.[6] In Deleuzean language, the propaganda model identifies the barriers, lines or 'striations' that determine what flows through commercial news channels and what does not. Herman, Chomsky and McChesney (Chomsky 2003; Chomsky and Herman 1988; Herman and McChesney 2001) have suggested that the machines of news production act to limit the flow of any information that undermines the continued flow of money. Specifically, this means that the news flows that do emerge protect the interests of the rich, the interests of advertisers, the interests of the powerful and the interests of the state. The flows of information that intersect with the interests of capital are amplified, whereas flows that undermine the interests of capital are diverted, recoded and reterritorialised.

The propaganda model of news production reflects the Deleuzean notion that heavy striations in an assemblage can channel flows of desire, and prevent lines of flight from escaping that same assemblage and having a chaotic effect. While news is a machine with the potential to generate flows of information for public enlightenment, it is also a machine with the potential to diffuse public tension and support and entrench the operation of power. The state news machine – what we call urstaat news – is news that is 'fixed in place', channelling flows according to expectation and established format. For Deleuze and Guattari, the 'rigidity' of any process is the thing that forms an apparatus of capture and repression, such as the way in which the Freudian Oedipus complex judges every person according to a universal, predefined set of neuroses. In many ways, Herman and Chomsky's explanation of news production serves to explain the problem with a centralised and generalised approach to news production. Such an approach needs to begin from a pre-existing notion of what is good for us, which assumes our interests prior to asking us and renders the consumer neurotic.

Herman and Chomsky make the point that the mass news/advertising assemblage amplifies certain flows of information and filters other pieces of information out of the flow. In the first instance, as Habermas notes, the news assemblage has long been synthesised with the advertising assemblage, and this has a serious effect on the content and expression of the news. The fact that so much of the news is about meeting the need of advertisers to extract revenue from the audience results in a lack of news that is critical of advertisers and their goals. Instead, the news assemblage has a vested interest in not only promoting and defending advertisers' products, but also in providing a flow of content that promotes passivity, consumption and visceral thrills in the place of informational and critical content (Herman and McChesney 2001).

Another barrier to the flow of news production has also been the cost of producing that flow. Historically, the expense involved in producing a newspaper or television news programme means that news tended to be produced by those who are already wealthy. Given these owners and companies have already constructed their machines around profitability, there is little reason to believe they would run their media machines any other way. We can understand cost as being a machine which facilitates the superposition of capital – those in command of massive flows of money, who have become accustomed to understanding things in terms of money, are more likely to organise the news machines around the flow of money, rather than the flow of information. More importantly, they have the power to prevent flows of information emerging that might challenge the interests of the wealthy.

Another control over the open flow of news information that Herman and Chomsky identify is the sourcing of information. In the day-to-day process of acquiring news, journalists establish their own flows of information from trusted sources and institutions who are seeking to create their own flows. Hermann and Chomsky suggest that this process of connection both forms along pre-existing lines and tends to develop into a habit, line or barrier of its own. For instance, when writing about the justification for a state decision, it is always easy for a journalist to find the lines and locations of state knowledge, while it is much less easy to forge general connections with resistant and minority communities. As a result of such sourcing, the official version of events is the most prominent represented in news reporting.

Similar 'channelling' of flows can be seen in the flack and anti-terrorism filters. Here, the news machine selectively restricts any news that may be seen as challenging to the state, or the dominant elements of the state apparatus. The Deleuzean conception of the state-as-concept (urstaat) is particularly useful in coming to grips with how this sort of censorship operates. In terms of flack, the news resists spreading information flows that might upset the dominant and large social interest groups. Instead, the news operates as an endorser of majority views, of a democratically sanctioned groupthink. The unquestioning condemnation of feminism, unionism, communism, terrorism and all other great evils works to ensure that the state's order words remain unchallenged, that the news presents a coherently repressing picture of the world as the dominant power thinks it should be. The state and the majority are understood to be ineffable, beyond reproach and beholden of the right to all forms of power.

Large-scale 'media events' are also formatted to make sure that they meet our preconceived expectations of our roles and the roles of the media. Dayan and Katz (Dayan and Katz 1994) highlighted how spectacular media events serve a ritualistic role in helping to define mediated cultures. High-exposure media events such as the Olympics, political assassinations, terrorist events and royal weddings are identified as significant enough to make the watching and reading of the event a major cultural artefact in itself (Dayan and Katz 1994). Such events can be understood as cultural rituals whose representation in the media carries a message about how we should understand ourselves. Each ritual requires a certain mode of representation and interpretation, which in turn creates a shared identity for our community. For instance, the glorification of national athletes at the Olympic games is exactly what reminds us of our national identity and re-creates our nationalism by promoting a nationalistic understanding as the only understanding, rendering any alternatives as deviant, or even seditious. According to Dayan and Katz, in a mass-mediated world the very ritual of consuming the media becomes a form of social integration (Dayan and Katz 1994, 15). The representation of these events forms a series of order words, which serves to integrate our perspective as commensurate with that of the state.

Occasionally, a flow might produce something that threatens the state, such as a flow of refugees or a flow of revolutionary ideas, but the news is always there 'to bring us back down to earth' and reterritorialise those lines of flight. We might have understood the moon landing as the first step of a revolutionary flow of escaping the earth and the state, but the news was there to remind us that it was about the US winning the 'space race', ensuring its technological superiority over other states. Alternatively, we might see the actions of Al Qaeda against the World Trade Center as a deterritorialised act of resistance to global capitalism; the news is there to remind us that Al Qaeda represents bloody insanity, and locates its territory somewhere between Afghanistan and Pakistan, possibly Iraq. At all points, the media knows its role is to play the *pappamummy*, never let one thing be inexplicable, tie all events to an overarching narrative of father/state superiority and render the consumer a placid and enamoured observer. And underneath all of this sits the Oedipalising delivery of broadcast news. Here are your experts, they must necessarily appear older than you, or at least more indentured to the way things have to be. They will tell you about this way, disguising their orders with a strong sense of inevitability and matter-of-fact objectivity. The deep certain voice of daddy is complemented by the soothing gentle voice of mummy. In comparison, you are rendered a child, naive, wide-eyed, in need of guidance. Your learned state of confusion and ignorance is just what the advertiser ordered because when you come across the ads, *you* become the daddy; here you CAN have power, with no end of supplicants ready to engage with your desire, based upon what you lack. The news produces us as infants beholden to the power of the state, which dovetails nicely with advertising that makes us feel like powerful little children.

News and the nomads

Of course, it doesn't have to be this way; people who share information often play a heroic role. The history of journalism is storied with the heroic tales of individuals and organisations who have remained steadfastly committed to spreading information even when it does not conform to the interests of the urstaat. Similarly, there are those who issue their order words with such awareness of the situation they are in that they speak of a 'becoming-other', communicating a transformative experience of haecciety. News everywhere has always had such 'nomads', who insist, following Hunter S. Thompson's advocacy of 'gonzo journalism', on inserting their own perspective into the story, making things up and resisting the supposed objectivity of their order words. The operation of nomads is always to latch on to what is happening but re-present it as something other than the urstaat-sanctioned unfolding. This form of news often looks like the news machine but remains guided by a different organising principle, which gives rise to a different machine.

> Even though the nomadic trajectory may follow traits or customary routes, it does not fulfil the function of the sedentary road, which is to parcel out a closed space to people, assigning each person a share and regulating the communication between shares ... there is a significant difference between the spaces: sedentary space is striated, by walls, enclosures, and roads between encounters, while nomad space is smooth, marked only by 'traits' that are effaced and displaced with the trajectory... the nomad distributes himself in a smooth space; he occupies, inhabits, holds that space; that is his territorial principle. (Deleuze and Guattari 2004b, 420)

A roll-call of some of the better news nomads of the past fifty years would include Thompson and his ilk, but also comedians, satirists, teachers and storytellers who have been able to reshape events in such a way that they engage with our self-affirming capacities – to laugh, to question and to really think through the experiences they are relating to us. The trick they employ is to begin by questioning their own subject position, by making it clear that the experience of the story is the thing to be earnestly considered, not the telling of the story. They are 'outlandish', the term from which Deleuze and Guattari derive their concept of 'deterritorialisation' (Deleuze and Parnet 2012). To 'deterritorialise' is to escape from the codes of the urstaat, to become nomadic.

Nomads also occasionally appear in the news in the form of 'the unexpected' that gains attention because it is so unexpectedly relatable. Gadi Wolfsfeld writes about how the Palestinian cause was given some sympathetic news coverage during the 1987 Intifada (Wolfsfeld 1997). Here, the Israeli state's story of a dangerous Palestinian threat was incommensurate with the vision of Palestinian children throwing rocks at the Israeli tanks overrunning their homes. The images were simply irreconcilable with the story the state had told, and thus, Wolfsfeld argues, the state news machine was momentarily unable to truly 'reterritorialise' the news. When nomads appear like this as news they provide moments of flow-escape – eruptions of contextual truth which, just for a moment, illuminate the machines of oppression and show the order words as they really are.

Watching the gates

Nomads are always allowing flows to become more or less revolutionary by preventing them from being channelled and filtered like the 'flows' of normal news. One of the most prominent contemporary examples of this can be seen in the rise of 'nomadic news', that is, journalism that is eminently personal and generally disseminated with no interest in making money. In the first instance, such 'citizen journalism' eliminates the need for the mass media assemblage and its filters of cost and advertising. It reinserts, instead, the capacity for more 'gonzo journalism', speaking truth to power and multiple perspectives on a single issue. Thus, while a journalist with 'radical' (radicle) thoughts might not be published in *The Urstaat Times*, that same journalist may publish through his or her own personal news service, be that via a website, blog or social networking service. The flows are thus 'set free' to some extent.

This news nomadism is resulting in a trend toward collaboratively edited and composed news sites, where it is no longer up to a centralised editor/producer to decide what is 'fit to print'. Instead, editorial decisions and amendments only take place after publication and they are made by a multitude, not an individual. As Axel Bruns points out, this doesn't necessarily mean that news is emancipated from social myth, advertising and public relations, but it does make the web of order words (along with perspectives, sources, popularity) more transparent (Bruns 2003). At all points we will find that these nomads are not enough in themselves to create new forms of news, as the urstaat news machine still controls so much information. The tools help, but they still need to be wielded with intent to disrupt the normal flows of information.

An instructive example of the conflict over order words between the community and the urstaat can be seen in the case of Aaron Schwartz. Schwartz was an internet wunderkind who, among many other achievements, helped develop RSS (Real Simple Syndication) – a tool for allowing people to cultivate their own news feeds – along with reddit, a news aggregation site that collects and ranks news items according to community interests and feedback. Schwartz also fought against the striated nature of information control. He was involved in the creation and promotion of a more liberal approach to intellectual copyright called 'creative commons'; he was also instrumental in accessing, and then making freely available on the web, books and court documents whose costs otherwise disadvantaged the poor.[7] He attempted to do the same with over four million academic articles that had been written for the sake of advancing knowledge, and were highly subsidised by taxpayer's contributions to education, but which were locked behind a paywall that prevented public access. However, the US Federal Government charged Schwartz with thirteen different felonies, threatening him with up to thirty-five years in prison. Faced with being branded a criminal for his actions, Aaron Schwartz committed suicide while awaiting trial, at the age of twenty-seven. His death received an objective mention in the urstaat news, making an example of the criminality of sharing information without asking for something in return. However, the news of his death spread through nomadic news sites like a rhizome of sympathy. The case highlights the struggle information faces to escape control. Even when it's free, it is still bound by order.

Watergate and WikiLeaks

One of the most famous incidences of the disruption of state power by information is 'Watergate'. Interestingly, this story has more to do with leaks than gates and it seems an historical accident that every 'non-state-sanctioned irruption of news' since has been appended with the word 'gate' as a result. We've since had our Camillagate, Monicagate, nipplegate, climategate, utegate,

Tigergate and so on, ad nauseam. The original Watergate was the office building where some of Richard Nixon's staff were captured by the police while conducting political espionage against the US Democrats. This disaster for the Nixon government was activated by the perfect assemblage of some determined journalists, a robust US Supreme Court (who ordered the release of White House tape recordings against Nixon's wishes) and a series of 'leaks' of information. The process was romanticised in *All the President's Men* to suggest that heroic journalists Woodward and Burnstein managed to remain committed to their principles, resist intimidation and bring justice to the system. However, the whole affair proved nothing more than that the state always manages to salvage its own legitimacy. As soon as the government agents had been caught, the state needed to absolve itself by claiming to be able to 'solve the problem' of the corruption of office bearers. In essence, after the scandal broke, many things happened, but nothing changed – Nixon even received a presidential pardon from his successor Gerald Ford. French theorist Jean Baudrillard argues that Watergate was a simulation of journalists serving up political justice, which helps the state by insisting that the 'system works' while taking our attention away from all the ways it simply does not work (Baudrillard 1994). Deleuze's response to Baudrillard would probably be to suggest that we shouldn't just notice that the Watergate scandal didn't produce justice – we should notice that the scandal continued to produce injustice in the form of the corrupt state and political practices that have soldiered on. A 'gate' is a suitable term, as it allows the controlled irruption of elements of the information flow, all the while ensuring the flow continues in the way the news machine dictates.

The reactionary attitude of the state towards leaks and flows can be seen in the collective action of states against Aaron Schwartz, as well as other famous leakers such as WikiLeaks, Edward Snowden and Chelsea Manning. The news these people release is not urstaat-sanctioned news and it often betrays the order words of the state. In fact, such leaks have shown repeatedly that the state is fallible and somewhat insidious, and those who leaked them have been punished remorselessly as a result. Chelsea Manning received a sentence of thirty-five years for opening up a flow of information about civilian deaths perpetrated by the US army; at the time of writing, Edward Snowden is hiding somewhere in Russia for revealing that US and UK governments have been secretly spying on their own citizens; Julian Assange is living in Ecuador's London embassy under diplomatic protection for his role in releasing hundreds of thousands of leaked government and corporate documents through WikiLeaks. All three of these people live with no suggestion that they will ever be able to resume normal life and no promised protection from their 'father/land'. The message here is clear: no one should speak of the mistakes of the state. The state, by definition, is infallible and all-powerful. Journalists need to understand this implicitly – but so do citizens. The state, after all, is watching you.

Press release journalism

Instead of pursuing a BwO of 'news that people don't want printed', urstaat news has become more focused on printing the flows of information encouraged by capital. Under the conditions of extreme pressures on their profit margins, with declining staff and less and less time to work on stories in the 24-hour news cycle, news has maintained its flow through providing for the 'release' of public relations and advertising material. Large machines – companies, organisations, states – produce and disseminate their own order words free of cost to news machines. In an effort to continue to command the flow of information (and the flow of money that accompanies it), news organisations are increasingly turning toward practices such as native advertising and press release journalism, which maintain their control over the news machine, even while only printing what people want them to print.

Press release journalism – the practice of printing press releases as news – has always been an element of journalistic practice, but has been exacerbated since the rise of digital technology and the corresponding changes to the assemblage of news production. With the 'always on' nature of internet time, decreasing revenues from sales and advertising and, of course, decreasing employees at news organisations, there is less and less time to write and check stories before publishing them, meaning that well-crafted pieces of press release journalism are getting published without any editing whatsoever. In Australia, it is estimated that the ratio of journalists to public relations employees has shifted from 1:1 to 1:4 in the past twenty years. Worldwide, quantitative research has indicated that around 80 per cent of news articles are directly attributable to press releases (Cameron, Sallot and Curtin; 1997 Shin and Cameron, 2003 Simmons and Spence; 2006). To put it in Deleuzean terms, the assemblage of news production and the flow of information have radically changed. Now that everyone can be a producer of order words for public consumption, the very notion that the news machine has a BwO oriented toward telling stories powerful people don't want told seems somewhat antiquated and totally inimical to the way the flows are currently structured.

Instead, urstaat news is capitalising on the flows of information generated by other machines, taking advantage of its relatively large and passive audience and its use of the authoritative (daddy/mummy) voice. One of the ways it is doing this is by acting as a mouthpiece for the urstaat and capital. For the former it operates as a kind of public service announcement, able to bring the audience access to the politicians and celebrities that are otherwise unreachable, and thereby reinforce the flows. For the latter it provides authority through devices such as 'native advertising', which is the printing of advertising material as though it were a news story. In this way, consumers can be issued their order words by someone that they trust, with the increased likelihood that they will listen and obey.

Refrain: What does digital news produce?

Digital technologies have introduced a series of schisms that have dramatically transformed the news machine and undermined the ability for the state to impose control over our news flows. However, while our points of connection are multiplying excessively, the news we seek out does not necessarily become multiple or nomadic. In fact, the assemblages of the internet and social networking are always finding ways to reterritorialise our interests and impose order words. Social networking will tell you 'these are your friends; this is what matters', recreating a little mini-state that re-enforces your preconceived notions of normality and importance. Meanwhile, search engines will continually inflect that your subjective world is actually objective. As Eli Pariser has pointed out, the great danger in the world of internet searches is that the users seem to think that they have found the information when, in fact, the information is shaped for them, given to them with incredibly complicated calculations of exactly which order words will work for them (Pariser 2011). What this means is that despite the prevalence of schizes possible with the digital information machine we don't necessarily escape the order of the urstaat, or the flows of capital (Harper 2011).

How to interpret all of this? Consider the origin of news as the origin of 'order words' – that is, communication which seeks to address the collective – and relate that to oneself. The evolution of the news machine has proceeded through the stages of the symbolic, despotic and then capitalist state. In the symbolic stage news is used to reterritorialise flows of desire upon the body of the warrior-king, in the despotic stage news reterritorialises flows in the interest of the state and in the final instance news reterritorialises flows in the interest of capital, that is, in the interest of flows in and of themselves. While this has led to a profusion of flows of news – blogs, posts, collaborative reporting, specialty sites – it has not necessarily led to a more enlightened reading public. Why is this? Because the thing that makes this machine work is still desire, and, as desiring machines, the news-consuming public tends to remain highly Oedipalised: that is, they refuse to think differently about what their authority figures tell them. What am I interested in? What does daddy tell me? Instead of information about climate change, I am given an endless list of global celebrities to endorse. With sporting codes and film stars, there is an entire system supporting my interest in what Kim Kardashian has posted on Instagram, and near complete silence on who my government killed today.[8] And understand it isn't that I can't think of new concepts beyond simple Oedipal desire, but everywhere capitalism understands that as long as I believe in Oedipus, I will never actually desire anything new, different or revolutionary; I will remain caught in the trap made specifically for mummy, daddy and me. As a result my desire to connect with others – to emancipate desire itself and to produce new flows and lines of flight – can be captured and re-internalised as the search for mummy, the trust in daddy and my relation to those two identities.

CHAPTER SIX

Advertising

It is at work everywhere, functioning smoothly at times, at other times in fits and starts. It breathes, it heats, it eats. It shits and fucks.

(DELEUZE AND GUATTARI 2004a, 1)

Desire, Deleuze and Guattari argue, makes the world as it is. It should be understood to be the basic 'current' that composes the world as it flows. Rather than see desire as the result of lack – as both Freud and Lacan have suggested – Deleuze and Guattari suggest desire is an innately positive force that seeks to propagate and create; the term they use for this force is 'desiring-production'.[1] As noted in the first chapter, desiring-production can be understood to be the essential pervasive force of life everywhere; all organs, all machines, are oriented by their desire to produce and, at the same time, give rise to our social and technological formations. Whereas Marx argued that to understand the world you must understand that the machines of production shape our world, Deleuze and Guattari's contribution to that idea has been to suggest we must also examine how these machines channel and harness desiring-production. It is possible to suggest that the state-led experiments in Marxism conducted in the USSR and China made Marx's mistake – believing that a socialisation of the tools of production alone would create an emancipated society. However, Deleuze and Guattari's position suggests that in these experiments they forgot to account for desire. The poor old Russians thought they didn't have to care about desire, and so they sought to control and repress it everywhere, in an effort to keep it contained within the state. They may as well have sat on the beach and commanded the tide not to come in. The capitalist states – led by the USA – did a much better job of using desire by plugging it into their productive machines, giving it an outlet, providing extensive objects of desire and encouraging that desire to become productive. During this time the US perfected the construction of advertising and marketing machines that could harness desire, which had the triple effect of stabilising the state as the arbiter of security for wealth, producing wealth through stimulating production and constructing a lack of consumption and wealth as a lack of fulfilment. What a victory for freedom.

Deleuze and Guattari's work begins with the assumption that machines can't function without harnessing the productive elements of desire and this is never more evident or true than with media. If it weren't for desire (desire to express, desire to reason, desire to persuade), we wouldn't have invented these communicative machines – words, languages, bibles, books, newspapers, web sites are all such machines – which were created as a sort of recording of particular flows of desire. Nothing makes this more obvious than advertising, which is aimed directly at utilising and manipulating desire; it is entirely focused on producing affects (Smith 2012, 186). This chapter will highlight how advertising, like news, has undergone a transformation to such an extent that advertising almost isn't recognisable as 'ads' anymore but remains at work everywhere. In fact advertising and marketing's crucial role as the productive heartbeat of communication has never been more certain or more powerful. First, we'd like to explore desire's potential as both a generative and repressive force, as this is the key to understanding Deleuze's approach to the function and future of advertising.

Desire or desiring-production?

Deleuze's conception of desire as productive lies somewhat contrary to how desire has been theorised by Freud, Lacan and most other psychoanalytic theorists, who understand desire as arising from an absence of something – a lack. Traditionally, desire has been generated in advertising by leveraging this feeling of lack. Sales and marketing departments are always feverishly at work making you want the thing you don't have by showing you how much less you are without it. Desire is seen to proceed through a series of stages, starting with the feeling of incompleteness: you start by feeling incomplete compared to what surrounds you, you then identify something symbolic of that transcendent thing you lack – such as beauty, wealth, power, respect, love – and you acquire it in an attempt to satisfy yourself. Finally, realising that what you have acquired does NOT actually satisfy you, you begin again by desiring the next thing (Deleuze 2001, 101–2).

On the other hand, Deleuze argues for a different conception of desire: as positive, as opening up the possibilities for new connections and new flows, and as inherently productive.

> What we desire, what we invest our desire in, is a social formation, and in this sense desire is always positive. Lack appears only at the level of interest because the social formation (the infrastructure) in which we have already invested our desire has produced that lack. (Smith 2012, 186)

To avoid confusing desire/production with desire/lack, Deleuze and Guattari use the term 'desiring-production' in *Anti-Oedipus* to remind us of the positive, co-creative relationship between the affective (desire) and the material reality (production). In order to understand the difference between desire and desiring-production, it is helpful to think first about sexual desire and production. Deleuze lauds an Ancient Chinese guide to making love, which indicates that true lovemaking does not involve racing to orgasm (vanquishing the lack) but rather appreciating the opportunities and options that each moment presents (exploring the event) (Deleuze 2001, 98). He states that the Freudian/Lacanian error is to believe that:

1. You will lack every time you desire;
2. You will only hope for discharges;
3. You will pursue the impossible jouissance. (Deleuze 2001, 102)

The problem with this formulation of desire is that it begins by assuming you lack something. To orient the process of making love around what it lacks means in some sense that the experiences presented are passed over in favour of the discharge, which also means that the participants are somewhat disinterested in the process and never really satisfied about what the experience produces.[2] You want a man because you lack one; when one arrives you hope only that you come too, anticipating that moment of multiple-simultaneous-endless orgasm, which, actually, will never come. You are thus exasperated and driven to desire more – you got what you wanted, but still feel dissatisfied because you understood your desire as lack.

Alternatively, Deleuze implores us to follow certain 'Oriental' cultures by understanding lovemaking as an attempt to reach a plateau, a zone of intensity that allows you to enjoy, embrace and assess your connections and your flows, an opportunity to make these things productive and endlessly positive (Deleuze 2001, 97–8). Plateaus don't release or exhaust energy, so much as carry it forward (Beckman 2013, 1). At these times you should:

> Lodge yourself on a stratum, experiment with the opportunities it offers, find an advantageous place on it, find potential movements of deterritorialization, possible lines of flight, experience them, produce flow conjunctions here and there, try out continuums of intensities segment by segment. (Deleuze and Guattari 2004b, 178)

Do all these things well, and you would 'have constructed your own little machine, ready when needed to be plugged into other collective machines' (Deleuze and Guattari 2004b, 179). This suggests that, given the appropriate appreciation for how your desire flows, and what it produces, you can figure out how to make that desire even more productive.

One can still have the orgasms, but it is important to understand that is not all that lovemaking produces. Moreover, when you have your orgasms, appreciate what they produce, not how they indicate lack! They produce flows of fluids, flows of affections, flows of disease and flows of life. Helen Cixous has even defended a positive understanding of jouissance – explaining the feminine multiple orgasm as facilitating a new stage of becoming multiple – casting the intense pleasure of jouissance as a productive becoming, a complete loss of ego. You can imagine these things. Your pleasure doesn't have to be dirty, or little, or even insatiable. The trick behind a positive experience of desire is don't think of what you lack ... your desire doesn't come from lack; think instead of what you produce as your desire is desiring-production.

Desire and advertising

How does this relate to advertising? Well, traditionally, media studies has understood advertising and marketing as harnessing desire as lack, and using the power of symbolism and imagery to make consumers peculiarly aware of what they don't have. Herbert Marcuse identified this 'manipulation of needs by vested interests' as perpetuating a 'comfortable, smooth, reasonable, democratic unfreedom' (Marcuse 1964, 1). According to a 1930s marketing trade publication, advertising 'helps to keep the masses dissatisfied with their mode of life, discontented with ugly things around them. Satisfied consumers are not as profitable as discontented ones' (Ewan 1976, 39). Consumer society catches people in a double bind for stimulating production; it ensures dissatisfaction with things as they are and presents an inadequate solution to that dissatisfaction. It creates ugliness and reminds people how intolerable ugliness should be, considering they work so hard. They should buy more – they're worth it.

> Although [the scientific and technical worker] has mastered the flow of knowledge, information and training, he is so absorbed in capital that the reflux of organised, axiomatised stupidity coincides with him, so that, when he goes home in the evening, he rediscovers his little desiring-machines by tinkering with a television set – O despair. (Deleuze and Guattari 2004a, 256)

At the very basis of Deleuze and Guattari's link between capitalism and schizophrenia is the profound dissatisfaction wrought by capitalist modes of production. Márx identified that capitalist workers are 'alienated' from their labour – they never get to feel pride or satisfaction because their production is only recognised by the 'discharge' of capital – and workers are rendered unfulfilled by, and out of control of, the process of production in which they have become a means to an end. At the same time, capitalism generates lack everywhere it goes, in turn giving rise to a desire for the things we can't have, control and fulfilment being two of the most marketable affectations in capitalist culture.

An important part of the success of this 'double bind' is the fact that most of us are thoroughly removed from the systems of material production. Ever since it catered to every material lack that we had, capitalism has tended to hide the material aspects of production in distant mines and sweatshops on the periphery of the world economy (Deleuze 1992, 6). Instead, ensuring the growth of capital has become a psychological exercise in producing lack, as corporations 'move away from structures producing goods and services ... towards structures, producing signs, syntax and – in particular, through the control which [capital] exercises over the media, advertising, opinion polls, etc.' (Guattari 1989, 137). Whatever it is that might give meaning to the subject (spiritualism, adventure, authority, relationality) it is all recast as something you could consume. As Guattari puts it, '[c]apitalist subjectivity seeks to gain power by controlling and neutralising the maximum number of existential refrains' (Guattari 1989, 139). Or, as Marilyn Manson noted in an interview with Mike Moore:

> ... the media wants to take it, and spin it and turn it into fear, because then you're watching television, you're watching the news, you're being pumped full of fear; there's floods, there's aids, there's murder. Cut to commercial: buy the [car], buy the [toothpaste].[3] If you've got bad breath they're not gonna talk to you, if you've got pimples the girl's not going to fuck you. It's a campaign of fear and consumption; and I think that's what the whole idea is based on. Keep everyone afraid and they'll consume. (Moore 2002)

In other words, advertising works by construing desire as generated by lack. Whatever is bothering you (and you should be bothered) can be fixed through purchasing (although you never will be fixed).

Oedipus – making you at home with your alienated self for 100 years

The profound dissatisfaction experienced by the individual under capitalism is, in the most fundamental sense, reflected in the profound dissatisfaction experienced by the Oedipalised subject. The Oedipalised subject is one whose psycho/social problems all return to working through his or her frustrations with family and failure to conform to an ideal model. Freud, the father of the Oedipus complex, identified elements of the story of Oedipus in a large number of his middle-class Viennese clients and came up with the transcendental notion that Oedipus rules the psyche.

The story of Oedipus Rex was first told by Sophocles in 429 BCE. It is a tale of a royal family torn apart by a prophecy that the new son would one day kill his father and marry his mother. In a bid to avoid this prophecy, the parents abandon the child, who then grows up ignorant of who his biological parents are. The grown son, upon learning of the prophecy from an oracle, flees his adopted family in an effort to avoid the prophecy taking place. In the process of fleeing, he kills a man who, unknown to him, is actually his true father. He then happens upon his original homeland, outsmarts a Sphinx that threatens the city and is awarded his original mother's hand in marriage, thus fulfilling the prophecy. When the tragedy is revealed, Oedipus's mother commits suicide, and Oedipus pokes his own eyes out, lamenting the inevitable and intractable nature of the fates and the humours.

Sigmund Freud saw this play performed soon after his own father's death and it apparently resonated enough with his own experiences[4] and those of his patients that he began to theorise that this 'Oedipus Complex' was at the base of all modern neurosis. He argues that our first, natural expression of our desire is to have sex with our parent of the opposite sex, but this desire is frustrated by our fear of our same-sex parent and, eventually, we learn to channel our desire into more productive, socially acceptable ends, eventually marrying an acceptable copy of our mothers/fathers and beginning the circle again. Our desire, in this typography, is always for what we can't or don't have. Our neuroses arise from our inability to properly reconcile our primal desires (you want to sleep with your mother/father) with our lived experience (this would cause a destruction of the family unit). Like Oedipus, our fate is always tragic, but Freud implores us not to run from our fate as Oedipus did, but to seek therapy to help us accept it.

Deleuze and Guattari recognise that while Freud may have recognised a neurosis that was particularly prevalent in the early twentieth-century Viennese middle class, he was highly mistaken in identifying Oedipal lack and neurosis as somehow universal, transcendent and inevitable. While there are numerous objections to understanding the world through Freud's Oedipal system, the one Deleuze and Guattari object to most consistently is that Freud 'took the transcendental path over the immanent one' (Buchanan 2000, 24). Where he could have examined desire as creative force that produces different things in different ways under different circumstances, he instead found a universal neurosis and repression that would always render the patient as 'lacking'. Deleuze and Guattari repeatedly describe the kind of 'reverse diagnosis' that Oedipal analysis imposes on patients. For example, they recount an incident where a therapist interprets a boy pushing a toy train into a tunnel as representing 'the boy entering mummy'. When the boy rejects this representation, the therapist repeats it until the boy surrenders, even though it casts a terrible pall over the feelings of satisfaction he might otherwise be enjoying (Deleuze 2007, 89–112; Deleuze and Guattari 2004a, 45). The same thing happens repeatedly and constantly with advertising and desire. The lack is created in response to an ideal that doesn't really exist, at the same time that the real source and product of your desire is neglected.

So Deleuze and Guattari see 'Oedipal thought' and capitalism as inherently connected. Each works with the other because they generate systems that thrive by creating lack. The consumer, as with the patient, will always be situated as lacking and his or her increasing immersion in the system will simply increase his or her neurosis.

[Capitalism's supreme goal] is to produce lack in the large aggregates, to introduce lack where there is always too much, by effecting the absorption of overabundant resources ... it alone doubles the capital and the flow of knowledge with a capital and equivalent flow of stupidity that also effects an absorption and a realisation, and that ensures the integration of groups and individuals into the system. Not only lack amidst overabundance but stupidity in the midst of knowledge and science ... (Deleuze and Guattari 2004a, 256)

Capitalism's genius in this regard is that it is able to harness desiring-production in a way that will never produce a limit or, if you like, a stasis. As opposed to more 'cyclical' world views such as Hinduism, Buddhism and nomadism, capitalism ensures that we do not seek balance, but instead are always dissatisfied with what we have. There is no longer any need for collective faiths, in fact, as our desiring machines 'are sufficiently filled with the floating images constantly produced by capitalism' (Deleuze and Guattari 2004a, 272). Instead, we are rendered as changeable beings who can be constructed as lacking in every space and subject position we inhabit – this changeability ensures that we can always be productive and we can always be profitable (Savat 2013, 57).

Capitalism, like Oedipus, works so well because it can always be used to 'decode' and then 'recode' everything. Anything that is considered meaningful can be given a price (given a prognosis) and then bought or sold (provided with therapy), according to a system of universal value that actually erodes the initial meaningfulness. Take the impact of capitalism on indigenous cultures, where once elements of physicality (inscription) or ritual (myth) were considered to hold power. Capitalism has undermined that meaning by making those inscriptions and myths worth money, so that indigenous cultures are now often prevalent because they are performed in a way (cultural tourism) that actually undermines their initial meaning. Oedipus has similarly stripped the inscriptions and myths of any meaning beyond the Oedipal code, creating a universal system in place of the particular culture. The myths maintain their value to the extent that they still produce belief and culture, and yet, at the same time, they are subsumed by the exchange of money that takes place in their performance; the money becomes the 'code' that underlies all the other codes, it becomes the one universal structure and flow. Like Oepidus, money always creates lack (one can never have enough), and it implies a universal standard for judgement.

It is certainly the case that the opening up of flows of desire enabled by capital is pregnant with profound and revolutionary possibilities. Take the transformation of the 'traditional' role of women in the European states in the twentieth century. The religious myth promoted by the Christian Bible is that women are largely derivative of men, carved from a 'spare rib' of Adam and grown to be an apposite and complementary element of man's existence. Their role was defined as being kept, being quiet and remaining, in some sense, the 'property' of men. These codes of meaning overhung existence and constructed resistance to change in the dominant political/public sphere[5] up until the point where the demands of capital – the need to harness the productive capacity of women in factories for war – were seen to override the strictures of myth. Again, this is a process of capital 'decoding' culture and myth. It is at once liberatory (look at what women can do now) and, at the same time, enslaving (look at what women lack now).

This movement of decoding can be understood as similar to a process media theorist Jürgen Habermas describes as 'the lingusitification of the sacred', where traditional views of the world lose their authority and are 'set communicatively aflow' by the decoding imposed by rational systems of money, property and political legitimacy (Habermas 1979, 178–205). However, while Habermas sees this 'freeing up' as a basis of optimism about the prospect of a more reasonable, sane and emancipated future (Habermas 1987, 344), Deleuze and Guattari argue that as long as we remain in the thrall of Oedipus/Capital, we will always be 'captured' by the neuroses that we find there. 'The decoded flows … submerge the tyrant but they also cause him to return in unexpected forms, they democratise him, oligarchize him, segmentalize him, monarchize him, and always internalize and spiritualize him' (Deleuze and Guattari 2004a, 243). As long as we remain Oedipalised and continue to understand desire as lack we tend to recreate our own tyrants, or find them in new places, with new faces.

Marketing is the new centre of the soul

The extent of capital's grasp on our psyches is in some way evident in the manner in which it perpetuates a system of value based upon the exchange value of signs, rather than the material value that Marx was so fixated upon. In this sense, the important element is how capitalism recodes desire: through producing 'signs, syntax and – in particular through the control which it exercises over the media, advertising, opinion polls, etc. – subjectivity' (Guattari 1989, 137). Deleuze continues this line of argument in 'Postscript on societies of control':

> This is no longer a capitalism for production but for the product, which is to say, for being sold or marketed. Thus is essentially dispersive, and the factory has given way to the corporation. The family, the school, the army, the factory are no longer the distinct analogical spaces that converge towards an owner – state or private power – but coded figures – deformable and transformable – of a single corporation that now has only stockholders. Even art has left the spaces of enclosure in order to enter into the open circuits of the bank ... Marketing has become the centre or the 'soul' of the corporation. We are taught that corporations have a soul, which is the most terrifying news in the world. (Deleuze 1992, 6)

Both meaning and production have been subsumed by desire so that capitalism generates exploitation in consumption and production in equal measure. The advertising and marketing industry is increasingly aware of how productive desire is and, as a result, is increasingly utilising consumer desires as a vehicle for their advertising. As such, marketing has already understood the importance of Deleuzean concepts and focused on making desire productive. This has involved an exposure of everything – history, culture, belief, subjectivity – to the flows of desire, investment and interest through capitalism's intrusion into every aspect of our lives. Whereas state capitalism sought to capture these flows and direct them to the benefit of the state, through taxes, armies and public works, we have moved into a 'new era' of marketing and anticipation of desire as a form of control, where the product is the 'ongoing process of production itself' (Savat 2013, 46). Deleuze and Guattari attacked this 'capture of creativity' in *What is philosophy?*:

> [T]he most shameful moment came when computer science, marketing, design, and advertising, all disciplines of communication, seized hold of the word concept itself and said: 'This is our concern, we are the creative ones, we are the ideas men! We are the friends of the concept, we put it in our computers.'

Information and creativity, concept and enterprise: there is already an abundant bibliography. Marketing has preserved the idea of a certain relationship between the concept and the event ... The only events are exhibitions, and the only concepts are products that can be sold. (Deleuze and Guattari 1994, 10)

Advertising has become the prominent social tool for understanding desire. Whereas philosophical thought and reflection may have, once upon a time, read desire as producing all kinds of revolutionary opportunities, advertising plugs all desire back into consumption, back into lack.

In every space we enter and every encounter we have, machines have sprung up to encourage us to follow our desire and make it consumptive. Consider, for instance, recent breakthroughs in visual analytics, which enable researchers to follow the movement of the human eye across a screen. This research gives real-time feedback about what elements of the screen projection catch the eye, and what elements lack interest. Once the 'tastes' of the eye can be discerned, the material on the screen can be restructured to take advantage of the viewer's attention and to trigger a greater immersion, a greater flow of desire. In truth, this is simply a further refinement of what has always been a concern of rhetorical persuasion – to understand the desire of the audience. This feedback is variously communicated by applause in the theatre, ratings on broadcast media and cyberanalytics on digital media. The trick here is the same: follow the desire of the viewer. Entertain that desire, make it flow, and you will be rewarded with the opportunity to make it consumptive. This is the secret of all advertising, however it is presented.

The Brave New World of digital marketing

Digital media has challenged the marketing idea that desire has to immediately produce consumption; instead it can produce simply more flow and it can become productive through the process of controlling the flow. Advertising and marketing in the digital assemblage is a great illustration of how desire is always converted into production/consumption; no matter where it flows, or where it ends up, it will always be reterritorialised into a productive machine. The idea of proliferating flows of desire is a central part of the success of all the new 'constructivist' forms of marketing. By 'constructivist' we mean approaches to marketing which have made the most out of the infiltration of capital into every aspect of our lives, or, to put it more objectively, approaches to marketing that account for the element of co-creation between marketing messages and consumers. In a capitalistic world it is not simply the case that the market manages desire and consumption; at the same time, consumers change the market through their consumption. As Dan Smith points out:

> I almost automatically reach for one brand of toothpaste rather than another, since I have a fervent interest in having fresh breath and cavity free teeth – but this is because my desire is already invested in the social formation that creates that interest, and that creates the sense of lack I feel if my breath is not fresh or my teeth are not white. (Smith 2012, 186)

Thanks to digital technology, marketing is able to discern how our desires are invested in the social formations we engage in, and make more certain than ever that our lack – of community, of security, of joy, of power – can all be made productive.

The move from marketing as inspiration to marketing as machine can be seen in two significant changes that have swept through advertising since the advent of digital media, both of which have Deleuzean resonances. The first of these is that advertisers no longer think of advertising as simple rhetorical persuasion but rather as a product, a machine in itself that can be used to generate and channel desire.[6] The second change is that the product itself needs to reflect an understanding of how to channel desire into a system that propagates further flows. You must have a strong brand, but your brand must also, in some sense, create new connections – develop its own territories. The goal of contemporary marketing is to make advertising itself 'useful, usable and desirable – as opposed to simply persuasive' (Vedrashiko 2014), where media designers seek to understand what motivates people to spread the advertising message – a process of harnessing consumers' 'active agency', or desire.

There is plenty of evidence in the vernacular of marketers to illustrate their militant orientation to surreptitiously change 'how things are for you' to make you produce for them. Marketing can be spreadable, targeted, stealth, guerrilla, clustered, tactical, strategic, viral or ambush; these names describing the processes through which the marketing machine stalks the prey of your desire. In some senses, this follows a lament that in a post-9/11 world, the uncontrollable element of risk has meant a removal of a real distinction between 'civilian' and 'military' spheres of war (Massumi 2009, 158). We are in a 'crisis capitalism' where the maintenance of the flow of consumption is a ubiquitous urstaat emergency. The same surveillance equipment used to spot suspicious packages left too long in airports is now being used to examine where consumers spend their time in shopping malls. Where do they dwell and what piques their interest (Crandall 2010, 73)? Every possible analytic tool is being used to establish an understanding of our desire. Once our desire is understood, it can be addressed, marketed to and made productive by those 'floating images' produced by capitalism.

The development of 'big data' analysis as part of advertising targeting is simply an extension of the attempt to constantly access and appeal to your particular interests, risks, concerns. The notion of 'targeting' the right consumers has been elevated through the powers of iterative databases and interfaces. Social media is the most obvious example. It is not just an extensive source of data on consumers; it is also an avenue for the promotion of advertising re-presented as people's 'interests'. Advertising experts talk about how lunch time is the new prime time, as advertising is spread via 'bite-sized' pieces of culture, which form the perfect material for consumers to pass on; their apparent idiosyncratic features make viral marketing content appear as the perfect expression of identity. Take, for instance, the 'NSFW (Not Safe For Work)' tag, which plays upon the idea that we view our desires as transgressive, at the same time as it recreates patriarchal notions of power.

Framing workspace media content as transgressive allows producers to acknowledge contemporary demands for professionalism and productivity while simultaneously validating a presumed need to take personal breaks at work. Thus, workspace media is positioned as the perfect content for personal breaks. The content is designed to counteract the effects of corporate drudgery by revitalizing an employee through entertainment.

> The less censored nature of the Internet allows workspace media production teams to push traditional boundaries in order to stand out in the crowded media landscape. Workspace media producers create irreverent content so that audiences can spend their break time transgressing social taboos within the safe confines of a conglomerate-owned website. (Tussey 2014)

By understanding how workplaces frustrate your desire, advertising agencies are seeking to make even the notion of being a resistant worker productive. As Homer Simpson states, the way to resist capitalist exploitation is not to join a union and strike but to show up to work and do a half-assed job.[7] The most important contribution contemporary workers in the developed world make to the economy is not what they produce but rather what they consume, and how they might generate further consumption. In this sense, the spreading of entertainment/marketing is one of the most important roles the contemporary worker plays for the economy. In the past brands used to seek to colonise cultural events and cultural products, but increasingly we are the product they are looking to colonise.

As it always is with persuasion, understanding the needs and interests of your consumers is paramount because, in many ways, you need them to feel as though their purchasing decision is a meaningful one, which they have arrived at because of their own needs and which they are willing to defend and sell. So, in order to get people to really invest their money, you need to make them think they aren't controlled. As the data collection on consumers becomes more pervasive, advertisers are able to discover how to overcome our ideological resistances to their messages and ensure that the right messages are targeted at the right audience at the right time and in the right way. Through this, advertising has increasingly become more innocuous, woven into the fabric of our very existence.

Capitalism has been armed by digital media to take great strides into understanding our tastes, our predilections and our secrets. Our lives increasingly leave digital traces – even our most private movements, activities, heartrates, purchases, friends, conversations and interests are being registered somewhere. And all of that data is used to generate an understanding of our desire. According to a leading digital marketing company, the collection of marketing data begins with:

... customer tastes, preferences and purchasing behaviour and third party data about median household income based upon location and workplace. Data [then] comes from a number of sources – the information connected by the data trackers themselves – including education data, information from financial products and services, retail, travel records; this is cross referenced against their data as acquired from other 'data partners' who also track your purchasing behaviour as an element of their marketing program. Finally, data is also collected by 'unbranded' partner data which are not necessarily 'owned' by a proprietary company but which is available by third parties which record your past purchases, behaviours, predictors, interests, geographic and demographic information. The result is that the database can present information such as 'people who are prone to buy "x"' and 'people who are likely to be interested in "y"'. (Perry and Anderson 2013)

What this data produces is a 'persuasion profile' that can 'generate implicit personas' or models of who you are that can be used to market particular products to you in the most effective way. According to the book *Dataclysm: Who We Are (When We Think No One's Watching)*, this kind of cross-referencing was enough for power companies to anticipate divorces with a 90 per cent accuracy, based only on the patterns of household power use (Rudder 2014). Digital media ensures a much richer data set, which isn't confined to one company, one web site or one person. Organisations such as Oracle, BlueKai and Axcicom will collaboratively compile data to ensure they assemble the most comprehensive persuasion profile possible for any given browsers based upon all possible information about them, allowing web sites to serve up 'a very targeted message' (Perry and Anderson 2013). BlueKai brag that such practices allow them to facilitate 'a 150–200% increase in sales via the campaigns that they constructed using big data' (Perry and Anderson 2013). What this kind of data mining promises to reveal about us, on such a large and broad scale, is essentially a persuasion profile which promises to understand your desire better than your own consciousness does.

This may seem like a moment of liberation, and in a very particular sense it is, because this concern for desire encourages it to flow, and as it flows it opens up the possibility of transgression, of a radical opening up of desire and an eruption of decoding flows. However, for three important reasons the use of desire by advertising tends not to produce any revolutionary transgressions. Deleuze suggests that the first of these reasons is the inherent difference between the production of marketing and art. Marketing, he argues, is only ever produced with the broader public in mind, whereas real art is *never* produced with the broader public in mind (Deleuze 2000, 369). In producing for the 'broad public', marketing always has to cater towards the most generalisable interests, tastes, ideas and preconceptions, whereas art, as a pure expression of desiring-production, is free to truly shock, disturb, experiment and produce difference as a result. Marketing therefore tends to 'normalise' our desires toward the largest average and most profitable engagements, whereas art (and desiring-production) tends toward more immanent connections.

The second problem is that we don't honour our desires if we understand them as coming from lack. If we don't escape our Oedipal shame, we only ever express the desire that we feel is socially appropriate. Take, for instance the use of 'private windows' in web browsing; what is it about our desire that we are ashamed of when we use private browsing? What aspects of our future do we not want to show up in our history? Do the institutions we have created not measure up to our fantasy? Is our desire for political change likely to result in terrorist charges? Are we afraid that our private choices might undermine our public brand? Private browsing and the desire to remove our digital actions from judgement is, in a fashion, a legacy of the Oedipal subject's continual interpellation as subservient, and an indication that we remain captured by a number of social machines.

The third reason our desire doesn't 'flow free' is that capitalism specialises in capturing desire and turning it into profit, even when that desire initially appears transgressive. Being cool and culture jamming started as acts of resistance to dominant consumerist culture, but were very quickly co-opted by marketing (Buchanan 2008, 25–7). Digital technology has enabled digital advertising and content to be shaped so exclusively to what appear to be unique and transgressive desires, removing any sense of resistance at all. Given the infiltration of the data mining into constructing the media you consume, you can find yourself in a situation where everything you see does nothing but confirm that your biases are true, your interests are universal and that there is essentially nothing in the world that conflicts with your understanding of it (Pariser 2011). That your desire may be 'captured' in this sense removes its possibility of producing things that are new and different. The more you can fit into an existing consumer profile (such as frustrated middle-class anarchist) the more likely it is that your desire can be plugged straight into an existing machine of appropriation. Instead of your desire becoming revolutionary, it is used to serve the needs, interests and production of those who have been able to 'understand' it. The more you conform to broad social templates of what you should want, how you should behave, the bigger you sit as a target for advertising interests. This troubles Deleuzean scholars who argue that when desire is made to conform to the interests of a dominant ideology (such as capitalism), it becomes essentially reactionary (Buchanan 2000, 29). It is caught, internalised, construed as lack and, while it remains productive, it only reproduces systems of repression. In its place we need desire which asks questions of power, which seeks to transgress social structures and create new connections.

Conclusion

Hopefully this chapter has made clear that while we can under-stand that capitalism and the advertising-of-lack is a sort of a trap, desire in itself is not the problem. Desire is a fundamental force of life and in essence is profoundly revolutionary. In many ways, the freeing up of our desire has generated a proliferation of flows that have eroded the durability of the state, tradition and discipline in general. Capitalism doesn't like things to stay the same; it needs to continually decode and recode meaning in order to continue to generate lack. It has to continually re-draw the production of our consumption. We may miss the ceremony and the spirit of ideological conviction, but we don't seem to miss the repression, the ideological war, the dismissal of difference, the subjugation of minorities and the occlusion of personal power. Capitalism, and more precisely advertising, has washed much of that away for us, leaving us with all kinds of opportunity to explore our desires. Some see this as an unequivocal advantage for humankind, while others see it as fraught with danger;[8] what Deleuze and Guattari stress is that we can't simply ignore desire but rather we must examine it, acknowledge its products rather than its deficiencies, and see what we can do. Desire, in and of itself, is unavoidably revolutionary: 'it is revolutionary in its own right, as though involuntarily, by wanting what it wants' (Deleuze and Guattari 2004a, 127). And this is, in some sense, Deleuze and Guattari's response to the neuroses induced by capitalism: don't fight your desires – embrace them. If you have a desire, it isn't because you lack, but rather because it can be productive.

In some ways Marx may have been right, capitalism might be producing its own gravediggers; 'capitalism's very facility for unleashing and containing change means that it is tapping into a highly unstable energy source, namely desire, which ... is revolutionary by nature, and is therefore extremely vulnerable' (Buchanan 2008, 27). And this is where Deleuze and Guattari situate the schizo as a revolutionary agent. For as long as schizos are able to follow their desire without thinking of what they are missing, they resist the neurotic Oedipalisation of repression, which guarantees the continuation of the feeling of 'lack'. The opening up of desire is not a bad thing, particularly if that desire transgresses social codes such as socially construed gender roles, attitudes to authority and judgements about normalcy and sanity. The revolutionary form of desire is that which is partial, non-specific, inclusive, non-restrictive, transversive and related (Buchanan 2000, 29; Deleuze and Guattari 2004a, 120–1). Instead of internalising your desire, seeing it as something within you, try to examine where it has come from and, most particularly, examine what it produces. At this point, don't try to understand what you want; as a single person, try to understand what your desire wants and examine, carefully, how that desire is created, how it flows, what it produces.

Given the complete inculcation of advertising into our world, and indeed the way that digital technology allows our worlds to change to suit advertisers' interests, the act of transversing social expectations and constructions surrounding your desires has become difficult. One way to do it is to think about the effect of your desire as a territory; wherever it flows, that is in some sense a part of your production, and a part, therefore, of your assemblage.

Go first to your old plant and watch carefully the watercourse made by the rain. By now the rain must have carried the seeds far away. Watch the crevices made by the runoff, and from them determine the direction of the flow. Then find the plant that is growing at the farthest point from your plant. All the devil's weed plants that are growing in between are yours. Later … you can extend the size of your territory by following the watercourse from each point along the way. (Castaneda 1971, 88; Deleuze and Guattari 2004b, 12–13)

The flow of your desire is productive: like the flow of water, it feeds some things while it erodes others (Knorr-Cetina 2007, 710; Savat 2013, 33). It is important to understand that the flow of desire is not the problem – it is where it flows and how it flows that really makes the difference. Does your desire for a new smartphone develop from what it would enable you to do, or rather from what you feel you lack without one? Do you desire the system of inequitable factory relations that are a part of its production? Does your ownership of a smartphone actually produce things you want, or is the production it creates in the service of your bosses, of international capital or other systems of repression? This understanding of what your desire is producing can help consumers think critically of where their desire comes from and what it produces. It is not only of what you lack, or want, but rather why you desire this thing, and what your desire produces along the way.

Deleuze and Guattari seem to suggest that advertising itself is not the problem; rather, it is a mindset that continually construes desire as resulting from lack. We are taught by states, by psychoanalysis and by advertising that we forever lack. However, it doesn't have to be this way. You don't lack – you produce. Why choose the transcendental notion that we all lack over the immanent truth that our desire always produces? (Buchanan 2000, 24). Deleuze and Guattari argue the only way to make the most of the irreconcilable elements that capitalism introduces into our lives is to forget about the reconciliation – follow our desires through the schizes they bring us to. Don't be neurotic about what you might be losing, or what you might be lacking. Instead, think only of what you are gaining, what you are producing.

CHAPTER SEVEN

Media content and audiences: Genre, difference and repetition

This chapter deals with all forms of media content as production: why we produce the media that we do, how the audience is configured and composed by media machines and, specifically, what effect digital media has had on the way the audience is conceived. In this chapter we initially seek to explain the way media machines relate to a particular audience by examining how genre relates to media production. Genre has always been understood to operate as a device for understanding the market for different types of content and is often used to answer questions about what content media should be producing. What kinds of people are going to buy a romance novel? Is political satire hot right now? Genre also establishes some 'boundaries' for content: a fairy tale should end up happily ever after, horror needs to be scary, and so on. Because of this, genre can be understood to be another tool for marketers to match content to audiences; as a result, it can be understood to allow capital to determine culture. Are you hoping to advertise to teenage boys? Then you should produce an action movie featuring cars and an attractive, scantily clad, female love interest. Such a 'use' of genre creates problems from a Deleuzean perspective because it is so 'generic'; it understands everything in culture through its averages and so only ever caters to, and recreates, 'the norm' in seeking to generate profit. And yet we often find it is content that transcends or transgresses genre that is the most exciting: take the success of a movie such as *Napoleon Dynamite* or a game such as *Depression Quest*. Deleuze's philosophy also explains how the repetition of genre can also be 'generative'. This chapter will seek to establish the ways in which the configuration of genre and audiences can 'capture' the creativity of media content, and the ways in which genre and audiences can be understood to lead to creative media content.

This chapter will also focus on the effect the digital media assemblage has had on media content. In the first instance, digital media has allowed for far more diverse constructions of media content than the mass media assemblage. By lowering the cost of production and evenly distributing the opportunity for media access, digital media has facilitated the development of ever more specific genres for ever more specific audiences, such as 'dark tearjerkers featuring a strong female lead', 'sitcoms about people who play online games' or 'lesbian Japanese rope bondage porn featuring dominant big beautiful women'. In all cases, the ability to construct cultural products freed from the arborescent flows of corporate media means that it is increasingly possible for minor cultures to produce and disseminate their own media.

However, while the ability to find a more specific audience and create more specific content is one of the most promising aspects of digital media, a close reading of Deleuze's ideas about difference and repetition suggests there are also some real dangers in the way genres and audiences are constructed by digital media. By looking at the problems that arise from understanding genre as a series of pre-existing concepts or representations, it is possible to explain what Deleuze feels is wrong with a concept such as genre, as well as present some of the more novel aspects of how we can engage critically and creatively with digital media. Contrary to initial appearances, there is much about the digital assemblage that renders media production more homogenised, more controlling; against these dangers, Deleuze gives us tools to cultivate difference, and, in particular, critical thought. At the very core of Deleuze's philosophy is a profound love for difference as a positive attribute, as something that sustains the utopian possibilities of thinking and creating. This understanding of the value of difference and the problems with the categorisations that threaten difference has become more and more important as the digital assemblage comes to determine media production. Understanding Deleuze's perspective on difference and repetition is key to figuring out how to make the most of the opportunity of the digital media assemblage.

Deleuze argues that differences constitute creativity and that representations such as categories, ideals and other general abstractions tend to reduce differences and thus limit creative potential. That is, the moment that we begin to use names, categories and genres to refer to things in our world, we fail to really appreciate them for what they are and we limit what they can contribute to our awareness. A simple way of understanding what this means comes from the Zen Buddhist story '*nengemishō*' (literally translated as 'pick up flower, subtle smile'). In this story a Buddhist master conducts a sermon in which he says nothing but simply holds up a flower before his disciples. While the majority of the disciples look on incredulously, failing to understand what is going on, one disciple, Mahākāśyapa, understands the lesson and smiles. Seeing the smile, the master knows the student had learned the lesson – that the all-important element of communication is not the representations (in this case the words), but rather the thing in itself, unique in the moment. This is recognition of 'the unrepeatable' that makes every experience pregnant with potential uniqueness. If the master had tried to describe the lesson he was relating, his words would have ridden rough-shod over the meaning – how can one appreciate the real intensity of a flower when one uses words like 'beauty', 'white', 'delicate'? While all these words help to provide an image of a flower they actually leave you with less than you would have if you encounter or imagine the flower yourself. Hence, the process of representation is flawed; what we actually perceive cannot truly be remembered, imagined or conceived (Deleuze 2008, 99: Hughes 2009, 74). To re-present something is always to lose something, and understanding the difference between the immanent (what is before you) and the transcendental (the concept that pre-existed) is key to understanding what you might be missing.

One way of understanding the implications of representations is to compare Deleuze's prioritisation of difference to Hegel's formulation of mediation (Hughes 2009, 85–7). For Hegel, apprehension is a process of understanding the real through a synthesis of ideals composed of binary opposites (a, not-a). If we wish to apprehend how much of an individual we are then we construct a 'continuum' between the ideal concept of individuality and its binary opposite (the ideal of communitarianism) and then we locate our individuality as sitting somewhere between the two points. By doing this, the mind employs pre-existing concepts as a way of understanding the world and, so, the synthesised 'thisness', peculiarity or intensity of the particular is actually overlooked in favour of a previously ordered and known world. This kind of synthesising thought, that always reconciles what *is* through a synthesis of preconceived ideals, undermines the ability to recognise and create difference.

As an example, consider the difficult issue of gender in gaming culture. If we follow the Hegelian construction of mediation, we see that girls are typically excluded from gaming culture because they are regarded by the gaming industry as 'not boys' – the pre-existing ideal categories of boy and girl are made important here, and established as the binary opposites. Using the Hegelian construction, we then seek to mediate the differences between girls as 'not boys' and boys. In doing so we tend to only focus on the ideal categories as opposites (girls like social games, boys like games about conflict) and in the process we recreate and indeed strengthen the original representations and the original differences. Even if we achieve a synthesis – let's create games that both sexes can enjoy – we have in essence really just reproduced the differences and tensions between the categories of boy and girl by making gender, and those categories, the origin of our creativity.

The idea that 'girls' pre-exist as a group of gamers is particularly useful for marketers, producers and critics; by creating media that 'buys in' to the primacy of the categories 'boy gamer' and 'girl gamer', they have created a hegemony of play to suit that notion, which, in turn, reproduces the primacy of the categorisation. That representation/image is likely to be unnecessarily reductive and unable to reflect the true 'variety' of gamers who happen to be girls, or who happen to be boys. The problem with treating 'girl gamer' as a pre-existing category is that you assume that the category should matter and in some sense recreate it when, in fact people's engagement with games otherwise has nothing to do with their categorisation as 'girls' or 'boys'. For instance, if we take the primacy of the category for granted we might start to say things like 'girls don't like games', 'girls don't play games', 'let's not make games for girls', 'let's not play games with girls'. The category of 'gamer' itself is a reductive representation, as it purports to include a wide array of groups who enjoy the experience of play and elides all sorts of differences in the process. The rejection of whole categories of gamers, as can be seen in the gamergate movement, highlights both the prevalence and pitfalls of a Hegelian approach to cultural production; but at the same time, it is clear that it is those who refuse to think in terms of such categories who really produce creative and innovative content.

Deleuze's alternative appreciation of difference is that it is differences, rather than categories, that constitute experience, and that experiencing that difference as a positive value is the key to unlocking your creative, productive potential. Categories arise from the constant repetition of events, but Deleuze's profound insight is that no repetition of an event is ever exactly the same, so the process of repetition only really highlights differences. This formulation is intended to make us more aware of the unique connections and intensities produced by any single event and less inclined to fall back on the generalisations produced by categories. So, he would suggest that rather than identifying girls as a contrary category of gamer (not boy), you should seek to experience the play experience of those games that so-called 'girl gamers' may particularly enjoy. When you find the difference, appreciate it as something that was created by the new connection you made, and which you can now experience in a process of 'becoming' a girl gamer. You can use the difference between that experience and your previous experience to produce new play experiences, new joys, new connections. The distinction is between pre-identifying what a girl gamer is on the one hand and seeking to experience what it is like to be a gamer who is a girl on the other: the former gives primacy to the category, whereas the latter gives a primacy to experience, and each approach represents a fundamentally different approach to what difference is. As Deleuze points out in *Difference and Repetition*: 'To fill a space, to be distributed within it, is very different from distributing the space' (Deleuze 2004b, 46). If you can appreciate each moment for its uniqueness and its thisness, its haecceity, if you can do such a thing without resorting to ideal representations and binaries, then you have a chance at creating something new. What you find about categories such as 'girl' in the meantime is that they don't exist as an ideal but rather an intensity, an experience of difference, for sure, but also something that changes according to the situation you are in, not something which always pre-exists your experience: not something you are, or are not, but something you can always become to a certain extent, in varying degrees of intensity – the category itself doesn't exist, but rather describes a state of being, a possible repetition and thus a possible source of difference.

Painting by numbers, culture within the lines

If thinking about difference and repetition at this point seems confusing, it is possible to recast the 'problems' with genre in the terms of Deleuze and Guattari's framework in *Capitalism and Schizophrenia*. In terms of desiring-production, the problem with creative media production arises when the flow of desire is restricted. As mentioned in the previous chapter, 'desire does not "want" revolution, it is revolutionary in its own right, as though involuntarily, by wanting what it wants' (Deleuze and Guattari 2004a, 116), and, as Buchanan explains, the problems with desire and its creations arise when the connections that desire can make are restricted, limited or closed off (Buchanan 2000, 24). The thing that restricts the free flow of desire in the theoretical formulations of *Capitalism and Schizophrenia* is the operation of machines that create lines (or what Deleuze and Guattari call 'striations') that channel the flow of desiring-production within territories. Striations are formed between homogenised components, both lines and spaces allowing for the distribution and flow of production (and therefore capital and power). The striations 'capture' the flow of our desire and direct it towards established ends, whereas the smooth non-homogenised territories allow us to shift our subject position, our intensity, flow and experience in a way that is commensurate with truly creative expression and thought. However, desire flows across a striated territory until it is confronted with a line and then tends to flow along it, toward the ends of the assemblage.

We can understand gender as being such a striation on the broad territory of biological life and humanity to form a further striation on that territory, also divided by the gender striation.[1] Within the human territory there are striations of greater or lesser strength dividing races, classes, nations, locations, interests and tastes, among many other criss-crossing lines that can be understood to divide desire. These are a series of lines delineating what kind of cultural territory one inhabits, created by numerous machines seeking to harness the flow of desire in that territory, in order to make it productive.

The depth and relative strength of striations are proportional to the layers of stratification that have created them, and these layers of stratification are again related to the strength of the machines (assemblages) that produce them, which constantly deterritorialise (presenting a moment of possible becoming-different) and reterritorialise flows of desiring-production, binding desiring-production back to an existing assemblage. The more that reterritorialisation conforms to existing striations, the deeper the striation becomes. In the past fifty years we have seen profound deterritorialisations in terms of race and gender that have smoothed over a lot of lines, yet it is difficult to argue that the line between male/female and black/white does not matter at all, what with assemblages of production, employment and privilege still reproducing those lines on the territories of the state, family and culture.

In terms of cultural production, stratification can be understood to represent the capture of particular creative expressions within particular genres and for particular audiences. In this formulation genres develop based upon the successful 'capture' of desire, and as that desire produces, the machine becomes more powerful, the striations more pronounced and the genre more defined. As Christine Geldhill points out:

> Each genre represents a body of rules and expectations, shared by filmmaker and audience, which governs its particular generic 'world' and by which any new entrant is constructed and operates. The task of the genre critic is to survey the terrain of this world, identify its *dramatis personae*, iconography, locations, and plot possibilities, and establish the rules of narrative engagement and permutation. (Gledhill 2000, 223)

Where creative production is pregnant with possibility genre provides an outline for a territory that retains, delineates and captures that production – a perfect example of how striations work.

The way in which cultural production is stymied by striations reflects the problems that Deleuze finds with the traditional conception of thought in *Difference and Repetition*. The mistakes of traditional philosophy include the following assumptions:

● That thought will always naturally tend toward 'goodness' and ideals

● That thought takes place based upon a prior model of thinking

● That representation in some sense takes priority over the natural in thought

● That knowledge is superior to learning in thought

These aspects of the traditional approach to thinking

> ... crush thought under an image which is that of the Same and the Similar in representation, but profoundly betrays what it means to think and alienates the two powers of difference and repetition, of philosophical commencement and recommencement. (Deleuze 2004b, 167)

The use of genre to define a territory for marketing and production replicates these assumptions:

● That all forms of group identification are naturally good and productive

● That cultural production is best based upon existing models or genres

● That genre can be understood to generate production (rather than the other way around), and prior categories are the ingredients of cultural production

● That conventions should always be adhered to so that the artifice appears more genuine

Every representation of thought tends to obscure its difference and its uniqueness, what Deleuze and Guattari call its 'haecceity'. The positioning of thought, genre, audiences, culture and so on as pre-existing the event and providing the 'ideal' for all further creation leads to a repetition without difference, and essentially positions culture as 'more of a sedentary locus than a trajectory of human development' (Hallinan and Striphas 2014, 6).

One example of conventions and representations in culture taking precedence over the immanent is the web site TV Tropes, which categorises every form of repetition in storytelling. The site provides an exhaustive catalogue of genres, narrative styles and devices used in the process of telling a story. These 'tropes' of genre are covered extensively from A: Abhorrent Admirer in comedy, through to Z: Zombie apocalypse in Horror. Each trope description provides a detailed 'model' of how that particular device is commonly employed in stories, with links to other tropes and examples of the trope as witnessed throughout popular culture. There are a number of inspiring elements to TV Tropes as a site – it is a community-based wiki that allows non-commercial usage of its material and it does offer a wonderful archaeology of storytelling. However, because it prioritises the model over the experience and attempts to classify and represent every aspect of storytelling, it also serves to further stratify and delineate creativity and consumption. As such it shows that even in a relatively rhizomatic system the particular 'model of thought' TV Tropes represents presents problems for creativity and experience.

The problems this can cause are possibly best described by TV Tropes itself in the trope 'TV tropes will ruin your life', where community members complain that browsing the tropes will 'merge surprise almost entirely with recognition' (Tropes). While the 'tropers' also celebrate the critical moment and higher level of engagement this familiarity enables, there is broad recognition in the community that placing the concept prior to the idea in some sense undermines the effect and immanence of the experience. By remaining transfixed by the category or the representation, you can become somewhat immune to the haecceity, the peculiarity of a thing in space and time.

But according to Deleuze there are even more problems with thinking about creative work in terms of representations (as opposed to situated experiences or affects). The first problem is that it is wrong to assume that becoming familiar with the tools of thought (knowledge, if you like) will inevitably result in an emancipative moment in its use. The problem with pre-existing knowledge is that it introduces the possibility of a certain 'idealism' being introduced to the concept. Take the trope of 'inspirationally disadvantaged' (Tropes) cited as evident in films such as *Forrest Gump*, *I am Sam* and *Rain Man*, where differently abled people are displayed as heroic savants who are invariably gifted in other ways. The trope, identified with the best of intentions, takes on an idealised life of its own, becoming the focus of future storytelling. The point is that even when the trope is satirised, such as in its description on TV Tropes and in movies such as *Tropic Thunder*, the attempt tends to further normalise the notion that all differently abled people are compensated by some kind of special ability. As Deleuze states, the process of presenting a contradiction (to the trope) only serves to strengthen the pre-existing concept (of the trope):

> It is only in relation to the identical, as a function of the identical, that contradiction is the greatest difference. The intoxications and giddinesses are feigned, the obscure is already clarified from the outset.[2] (Deleuze 2004b, 263)

The danger for media production lies not only in the possibility that these tropes become machines that determine future production but also in the sense that this repetition continually gravitates towards pre-existing concepts, causing deeper stratifications in culture and stymying the possibilities of difference. While tropes and genres allow us to experience a thrill of recognition, they can quickly become exclusive and determining, and therefore lacking the ability to creatively produce. It would be churlish to lambast the creators of categories such as those on TV Tropes for stifling creative thought when they are really doing nothing more than categorising the things they love in an effort to more intimately understand them. However, the kind of categorisation that happens on TV Tropes is occurring in a far more ubiquitous and insidious way through our use of digital media.

The digital mapping of desiring-production

As Eli Pariser points out so aptly, we are increasingly being categorised by digital media in ways that diminish our overall exposure to difference (Pariser 2011). The tracking of our behaviour through our digital traces means that we are increasingly divided into ever more peculiar and sophisticated categories. Before we consider how such a 'distribution' might work to deliver us more peculiar and sophisticated media, it is worth considering that the machines that generate these striations are predominantly those aligned with advertising and marketing. As mentioned previously, advertising 'works' by ensuring that messages are directed at the 'right' audience – those who are inclined to be interested in the product or susceptible to the message. As a result of this production, a large part of the work of advertising is seeking to understand the audience, so that they might be exposed to the right messages. This idea is as old as rhetoric: you need to understand your audience in order to know how best to persuade them, so the more you can know about your audience, the more likely you will be able to construct a message that will affect their behaviour. In the process, the message is shaped by a sense of what is commonplace and generally acceptable, relying upon established techniques, ensuring that the same motifs, the same themes and the same desires are re-employed, creating a stratified, rigid flow of desiring-production.

Take, for instance, an audience member who has shown a previous inclination for purchasing zombie movies. By analysing his or her online purchasing behaviour it is possible for a database query to highlight that this particular person likes zombie movies and is more likely to buy 'zombie-themed' material. As a result of the ability of databases to record this detail, and the ability of the interface to adapt to it, web sites that have access to this information can tailor their content/advertising according to this knowledge. And, as a result, the user is endlessly confronted with an internet experience that reflects his or her previous interests back – he or she sees more zombie content, more zombie products. Advertising also follows this rule. If I've shown myself to be a dog owner or dog lover through my purchasing or browsing behaviour, animal welfare groups can access this information and generate specific images, content and marketing materials based upon it. So, if I visit their sites, I would see a picture of a cute puppy, whereas other people may see a kitten or piglet, based upon their own data profile (Perry and Anderson 2013). As marketers become more familiar with our desires, they continually channel our attention towards the things that worked in the past, stratifying culture through ever deeper striations.

Online media services such as Netflix, Amazon, Steam and YouTube have the ability to construct an image of your tastes based upon your previous purchases, along with external data they can scrape up about you and any feedback you've provided from clicks, to time spent on a page, to comments and ratings. When correlated with the massive amount of data that exists about their other users' preferences, the algorithms run on these databases can return a highly accurate understanding of what you are also likely to be interested in (Hallinan and Striphas 2014). Pariser points out that by using such algorithms Netflix is able to anticipate how its users would rate over 1,000,000 movies, and it uses this information to decide which particular movies to suggest to Netflix users (Pariser 2011, 129–30). By doing this sort of thing well, media providers 'give the people what they want' and in the process increase the likelihood that the consumer will consume more.

This in itself should come as no surprise; successful advertising has always involved finding particular pieces of media content that will attract the correct demographic and psychographic audience. But in a clear illustration of how desire is productive, Netflix is also using its knowledge of what kind of content is most successful with its customers to create and commission its own content (Madrigal 2014). In the most positive sense this is about forging connections and enabling flow – understanding the audience means that you can cater more specifically to their interests, and, in doing so, create a situation where consumption is more likely to happen. However, this process can also ensure nothing new is ever created and no one ever experiences genuine difference.

This is the problem with this kind of repetition – the process of encouraging the desire to flow as it has before – is precisely that the striations that mark off an audience, genre or product are reinforced and, in a digital world, can end up affecting the process of production. The sudden, responsive appearance of material related to previous internet searches is one example of this; however, this behaviour is also evident in the production of news. The more 'clickable' a story is (a cat saving a baby's life, a fight between celebrities) then the more likely it is that the story will be produced and will appear again and again (Tandoc 2015). This process is working in all media: hence, for instance, the proliferation of digital games about being a gangster, soldier or sports star appealing to the appetites of a young, middle-class male demographic, and the proliferation of magazines for young women about fashion, celebrities and heteronormative sex.

The reason we see 'popular' content repeated is the profit motive that sits behind much cultural production. With the advent of big data, the production of content can be predicated on the mapping of an audience that is big enough to justify it. As Cindy Holland, head of producing original content at Netflix, stated in an interview with *The Guardian*:

> We have an immense amount of data, we see everything our subscribers are watching. We can identify subscriber populations that gravitate around genre areas, such as horror, thriller and supernatural. That allows us to project a threshold audience size to see if it makes for a viable [profitable] project for us. (Sweney 2014)

So the audience in its ideal form pre-exists the product: the audience is constructed before the product is even produced and the product is produced for the audience. This kind of production seems to preclude the possibility of difference emerging in content. The producers of genre already know their audience and so genres are creatively limited and determined as a result. The process of creating 'for a public' strips the content of any actual creative merit.

The elimination of difference is compounded by the use of big data analysis to determine what kind of content ought to be produced for the profitable public. The analysis of such large data sets introduces a tyranny of the majority through the law of large numbers, which essentially recreates the problems Deleuze understands to rest with the use of representations and categories. Simply stated, the law of large numbers suggests that the more data you have in your sample, the more the mean will approach the 'true' average. Or, the more data you look at, the less deviance you get from the average. If I ask two people what kind of porn they watch, I might receive a general answer that is a little bit unusual, say 'gay and black porn', simply because the sample is so small. However, if I ask a million people that question the answer will approach the global average: 'teen porn' (PornHub 2015). As such, the search for large numbers always involves an elimination of difference and, as noted by representatives of big data marketing companies, there is a natural tendency to gravitate towards the largest possible numbers when seeking to create profitable media content.

> We're looking for that high volume because again, as a marketer, you really want to look for audiences that are quite large in size just so all the effort that you put into your personalisation efforts can reach a fairly sizable audience rather than looking for a needle in a haystack. (Perry and Anderson 2013)

By prioritising the flow of profit, the creation of media according to previous generic success encourages producers to fall into all the mistakes of categories and representations. In doing so, the connective synthesis starts becoming limited in what it can connect to, indeed it is limited in what it perceives, and as such it starts to repeat upon itself, eliminating difference and producing a despotic culture, that is, one with more and more teen porn.

While the suggestion that Amazon or Netflix can predict with incredible accuracy what you will enjoy seems a fantastic development in terms of shopping; it betrays the fact that your actual experience of the decision is lacking, as your choice is based upon preconceived ideas and an 'ideal' synthesis of your previous behaviour. What it doesn't actually leave room for is the very subtle nuance, the aura and, of course, the unexpected. As Pariser points out, the repetition of our own desires actually limits our incentives to experience different things, because we are surrounded by things 'with which we're already familiar (and already agree), making us overconfident in our mental frameworks' (Pariser 2011, 89). And this coincides with the fact that what we are familiar with is always already being pulled towards the centre because of the problems of categorisation.

> From the standpoint of analogy [or algorithms], everything happens in the middle regions of genus ... in terms of mediation and generality – identity of the concept in general and analogy of the most general concepts. It is henceforth inevitable that analogy [or algorithm] falls into an unresolvable difficulty: it must essentially relate being to particular existents, but at the same time it cannot say what constitutes their individuality. For it retains in the particular only that which conforms to the general. (Deleuze 2004b, 47)

While television, and mass media in general, has always sought to understand our desire and make it productive, through ratings and sales information, there has always been a 'blessed ignorance' involved in discerning that desire. Some newspaper editors might believe they had a public duty to print certain stories, some writers might believe that their work had its own creative merit and some producers might stick with an edgy television show because they believe in the material, even if initial ratings were low. Now, digital media and big data means all of those beliefs must persist against the harsh appearance of the apparently objective and extensive average. And in terms of profit, the writer, the journalist and the producer are all looking for clicks and hits, and they all, increasingly, know what kind of content produces that flow. While the media has always been shaped for our tastes and our existing predispositions, the process of categorisation that takes place in digital media thus tends to obscure the 'edges' of our experiences, while at the same time transcending the architectural and immanent idiosyncrasies that might produce difference in more local media assemblages.

The positives of media and audiences

If there is a way out of this mess it is through recognising that the process of repetition can also generate an awareness of differences. In *Difference and Repetition*, Deleuze identifies that, once you remove the belief of the sanctity of pre-existing concepts, then repetition will generate a new awareness of the immanence of experiences. According to this formulation, we are endlessly confronted with the failure of our memory to properly reconcile our recollections with our direct experience. Whenever we experience a 'repetition', the memory we have of a thing never fully accounts for the thing we encounter. According to Deleuze's formulation of how thought happens, when we encounter something we initially apprehend it, our memory interprets it, and when our mind fails to perfectly reconcile the difference between our apprehension and our memory it produces our experience (Deleuze 2008, 64). This formulation is actually borne out by the latest biochemical research into the way memory works in the brain. When we encounter something, we tend to attempt to categorise it and, to the extent that we are successful, it becomes meaningless to us, eliminating its potential difference. Certain instances call on us to employ what are 'in essence' implicit memories – how to ride a bike, for example – when we are not even aware that we are drawing on memory (Kandel 2006, 132). However, when something 'different' appears – a bump in the road that throws us off balance – the brain gets to work creating new synaptic pathways and new concepts in order to deal with the divergence between sensation and memory. It is during this encounter of difference that new synapses are connected in the brain, stimulating new flows and new mental processes, making one more aware of the difference between balance and imbalance that was otherwise imperceptible. According to Deleuze's formulation, it is through the formation of these 'unchartered channels' that thinking takes place (Gaffney 2010, 279).

As outlined previously, this conception of thinking presents particular problems if we are always reconciling a static material world with a static world of ideal concepts, the problem being that our minds get stuck in an eternal repetition of the same, producing nothing new. But Deleuze suggests that neither the material world nor the world of concepts ever actually remains static. The material world is forever different due to the haecceity of the instance; the world of concepts is always impoverished when compared to the situation in which it is employed; the synthesis between real and ideal is never symmetrical, it is always born of a violent failure of the real to correlate with the expected (Hughes 2009, 87).

This failure of thought to successfully apprehend or recall the world is precisely what for Deleuze ensures that thinking will continually erupt. As Deleuze outlined in a seminar on Kant:

> ... there's a consolation; at the moment that the imagination finds that it is impotent, no longer able to serve the understanding, it makes us discover in ourselves a still more beautiful faculty which is like the faculty of the infinite. So much so that at the moment we feel for our imagination and suffer with it, since it has become impotent, a new faculty is awakened in us, the faculty of the supersensible. (Cited in Hughes 2009, 126–7)

Here Deleuze's conception of thought resonates with that of Hannah Arendt, who identifies that the thing that guarantees the continuation of thought is precisely the fact that 'nothing happens more frequently than the totally unexpected' (Arendt 1958, 300). For Arendt, this process can be encapsulated in the experience of giving birth to a new life, a process that ensures that humans understand both the limits of their control over their material world and also the impotence of categories when related to experience (Arendt 1958, 11, 247).[3] However, Deleuze is also pointing to the difference between imagining what an experience is like, which is always impoverished by the representation of the experience, and actually experiencing something (like parenthood) all the more deeply because you cannot imagine it until you experience it. In such a process, according to both Deleuze and Arendt, we are awakened to both our own limitations and also the infinite possibilities of the universe. It is at this point that we begin to think creatively because we are experiencing difference: we become particularly sensitive to the differences between the representation, the memory and the real.

Deleuze describes this moment of thought as defined by the absences of rules, essentially transgressive and open to chance, an 'aleatory point'. The act of thinking is a 'throw of the dice'; it does not operate according to an existing rule – it invents its own rules (Hughes 2009, 132). In the Deleuzean formulation of desire, desire attempts to resist capture and follow its own production. In terms of the creation of culture, it avoids falling into repetition of cliché and genre, and becomes responsive to immanent and local affects. And this is possibly the most optimistic outcome of the process of examining the way desire flows through the digital media assemblage. As Google search looks at 'what works', it is (in most cases) not applying an overarching 'moral code', but rather allowing desire to reveal its own structures. Google generally does not elevate any previous existing code above profit (and its correlate popularity), allowing it to be somewhat sensitive to desire. Some of the despotic and Oedipal overcoding remains – the general will always elide the different – but Google seems to only censor search results on the basis of audience response. This provides a far more 'de-Oedipalised' media experience for general users. For instance, the top result when we search 'watersports' is an urban dictionary entry defining it as a BDSM term for sexual play with bodily fluids, probably because it is one of the most popular and most profitable search results for that term. Even though we might be interested in surfing and diving, we are still exposed to these flows; they are not stifled by a reactionary overcoding. And such flow freedom has allowed the rise of some relatively unique internet subcultures, such as 'furries' (people who like to dress up as animals) and 'bronies' (men who enjoying playing with, and writing about, small toy ponies). It is argued that such 'marginal' cultures owe their existence to the existence of a non-Oedipalised and reactive medium such as the internet (and Google search) (Watercutter 2014). And, of course, the development of big data means that even the 'long tail' of marginal cultures can be sustained. So those people who are interested in bronies, or furries, who may otherwise be too geographically spread out to be marketable via traditional media can now constitute a group both large and accessible enough to be marketable on the internet. The eruption of difference around communities and connections that are specifically not for profit has enabled new flows to emerge and makes us more aware of the existence of difference. As a result, while certainly still striated by profit motives, the architecture of the internet allows for a far more diverse range of connections to be made if one is able to resist their own Oedipalisation.

Another apparent positive of digital media in terms of creative expression is the way the content of the media can transgress the boundaries of the medium. The ability to be mobile while engaged with media, the spreadability and persistence of information, along with the emergence of 'augmented reality' software and interfaces and, of course, the fast switching between tasks on digital software, all encourage a collapsing of traditional contexts and make it more likely we might encounter those 'bumps in the road' that make us think. According to danah boyd, the lack of spatial, social and temporal boundaries while using digital media makes it difficult to maintain a distinct social context, creating an experience where incongruent contexts are 'regularly colliding' (boyd 2010, 49–50). The opportunities that these collapsed contexts seem to present for transgression are multiple and chaotic; the ability to bypass parental control of communication is an obvious example of an emergent experience that requires new thinking. Similarly, it may only be a matter of time before NSFW marketing finds its way into an augmented reality experience, possibly transforming bosses and workmates into caricatures while satirising corporate communication, which may precipitate a raft of intransigencies. Such collapsed contexts seem to open up the opportunities 'for one to distribute oneself in an open space, according to frequencies and in the course of one's crossings' (Deleuze and Guattari 2004b, 530) in such a way that bypasses traditional constructions of authority, experience and genre in favour of the unexpected, the itinerant and transgressive act.

As we have already seen, digital media works broadly by allowing database algorithms to define your experience of the media. In this sense, and most importantly, the media themselves tend to re-enforce the primacy of the category over the immanent. In terms of Augmented Reality, the programmed experience overrides and elides the immanent one, and while it may well create a transgressive possibility it still imprints a detached, imperial and striated understanding of reality as an augmentation. The fact that advertising, news and even content will tend to be generated by media machines for the largest markets reinforces a 'centring' of general content, which is reinforced by a 'popularity divide' in technological developments. Simply put, while an augmented reality experience for bronies is possible, it will tend to only be created by media executives if and when an augmented reality brony market is identified as financially viable. Nevertheless, it is possible for the brony community to develop their own tools, construct their own augmented reality, for no other reason but to allow their difference to erupt. This is the step that suggests a true democratization of the media: when the central organising principle of media production becomes connection, expression and becoming rather than profit.

However, while digital media open up the possibility of encountering the aleatory point that will force us to think creatively, they are still limited by the limitations of the existing stratifications and the existing delineations. The digital network recreates the problems Walter Benjamin identified in 'The work of art in the age of mechanical reproduction', where the separation between audience and art leaves the artist unaware of visceral feedback from the audience, which impoverishes both the artist, the audience and the environment (Benjamin 1969).[4] In a networked society 'contexts often collide such that the performer is unaware of audiences from different contexts, magnifying the awkwardness and making adjustments impossible' (boyd 2011, 51). While it is clear that the internet does offer the opportunity for audience interaction, these are thoroughly delineated interactions that exclude the vast majority of environmental feedback. As Green and Jenkins identify, media all too often construct their audience as a series of organs without bodies: 'The consumer is an eyeball in front of the screen (in television terms), a butt in the seats (in film or sports terms), or whatever other body part media companies hope to grab next' (Green and Jenkins 2011, 111). Such a measured connection between artists and audiences can only reproduce the most despotic pleasure, and it precludes the possibility of the joy of the unexpected that is constantly brought about by the actually existing heterogeneous world, because the differences we encounter that force us to think 'dwell in dark regions, not in the temperate zones of the clear and the distinct' (Deleuze 2008, 64).

It is important to understand that the 'liberation' of the media is not actually linked to the technology, but rather to the approach to producing and consuming, and the architecture supported by the media's organising principle. One way of illustrating this is to show how transgressive media experiences and collapsed contexts can never actually produce difference – they can only make difference more apparent. For Deleuze and Guattari every social and psychological context is profoundly linked to the environmental context, and that environmental context is inextricably heterogeneous and potentially creative (Guattari 1989), whereas any 'overcoded' context such as that provided by media will tend to be more homogenised, more delineated and based upon a representation rather than the immanent environmental context. Nevertheless, we can make media a source of difference by 'plugging media in' to our immediate environments and becoming less concerned with the 'objective' world out there.

Pop music, which is constantly derided as both generic and exploitative, can actually provide an avenue for becoming public for an otherwise private individual, simply by providing an element of repetition in culture that can provide a sense of belonging and ownership (Buchanan 1997). Through the kind of repetition that makes one feel at home, even the most generic pop tune can encourage a creative subject position if one uses it to relate more directly, more sensitively, to one's immediate surroundings. All repetition can give rise to difference if you pay close enough attention to the local and immanent to see how the flows relate, especially making sure they escape the striations of the profit machine. All genres, even the most generic ones, and all audiences, even the most banal, are constantly producing difference when they are rendered as local and immanent. It is only at the macro level that the machine effectively homogenises culture; it is only when we treat the categories as pre-existing and ideal that we end up with more of the same. If we can contextualise properly, and forget the words and representations, and instead appreciate the affects for what they are, then we open up ourselves to difference.

Where to for creative media production?

Staying stratified – organized, signified, subjected – is not the worst that can happen; the worst that can happen is if you throw the strata into demented or suicidal collapse, which brings them back down on us heavier than ever. This is how it should be done: Lodge yourself on a stratum, experiment with the opportunities it offers, find an advantageous place on it, find potential movements of deterritorialization, possible lines of flight, experience them, produce flow conjunctions here and there, try out continuums of intensities segment by segment, have a small plot of new land at all times. It is through a meticulous relation with the strata that one succeeds in freeing lines of flight, causing conjugated flows to pass and escape and bringing forth continuous intensities ... Connect, conjugate, continue ... (Deleuze and Guattari 2004b, 178)

So what would we suggest to those who want to be genuinely creative in their media production and give rise to content whose difference will make people think? The first suggestion, made a number of times within this chapter, is to abandon the motive of profit. This point is critical. Instead, organise your production and consumption around different goals – community, connection, understanding, becoming – as profit will only ever help you to create more of the same. Replace the term 'profit' with the term 'production'. The real goal of knowing your genre and finding your audience is so you can become more aware of the differences within and between the two, and use those differences to create something new.

The second suggestion is not to abandon genre completely but encounter it as a territory of potential possibility rather than as a prescription. Don't understand genre as a category but rather as a potential intensity of affect. While depictions of genre and audiences are always flawed and missing something, their failure to live up to our expectations, or our memories, our imaginations, can make us more aware of their differences and become productive. As Christine Gledhill points out, the 'modality' or repetition provided by genre can actually help bring to light the subtle differences between cultures, historical trajectories and genres themselves in really creative ways (Gledhill 2000, 229). Moreover, the striations that are created by genre and audiences can actually provide a useful guide to the lines that need to be crossed in order to be creative.

> ... boundaries serve not only to separate and contain but also constitute meeting points, instituting contact between spheres the dominant culture seeks to divide. Definition through differentiation brings new terrain into view. Desire is generated at the boundaries, stimulating border crossings as well as provoking cultural anxieties. (Gledhill 2000, 237)

By understanding genre as a source of repetition that can give rise to difference, one can use genre as a template for truly creative media.

Finally, whatever media you use, have it plugged in to your immanent world. Forsake the 'objective' and 'transcendent' world out there and create and consume in a way that relates to your own experiences, your own particular world. The profit motive means media machines will tend to centre production around the tastes of the majority and as such will tend to create representations in the place of connections. Digital technology does not free us from the interests of profit-making – it just makes the representation of desire more sophisticated and all-encompassing. To generate difference from that engagement you must make the media you use your own. Make sure you understand how what you read, see and construct relates to your local and immanent world, instead of treating the media you consume as somehow pre-existing, transcendent and sanctified (Bogue 2007).

CONCLUSION

So how should we approach media after reading Deleuze? In *Anti-Oedipus*, Deleuze and Guattari attempted to describe a common method of analysis that would recognise the importance of difference and desire, along with the inevitable role of assemblages. They called this method 'schizoanalysis' and we would like to conclude by summarising how 'schizoanalysis' might be applied to the media. Schizoanalysis takes place through three simultaneous tasks – the destruction of existing assemblages, the mapping of desire and the production of new assemblages.

In the first of these tasks the trick is to destroy the old assemblages, to discard them in their entirety, rather than assume that there can be some amount of negotiation or working through of issues (Buchanan 2008, 117). As described throughout this book, the media has developed systems of interpolating and distributing our desire in ways that produce our own repression. In the process they have constructed a world of seamless control, of modulation that works so effectively because it contains our flows by maintaining them.

> [Such a] control is not a discipline. In making freeways, for example, you don't enclose people but instead multiply the means of control. I am not saying that this is the freeway's exclusive purpose, but that people can drive infinitely and 'freely' without being at all confined yet still being perfectly controlled. This is our future. (Deleuze 1998, 18, cited in Galloway 2006, 87–8)

Media under capitalism has developed an infinite array of methods of dealing with 'objections' and 'opposition'. Going to the mass media with a problem in the hope they might change something is like going to a lion's den with a baby lamb – all they see is something they can consume. Your problem will be broken down into socially acceptable representations, fed back to the people in a way that won't upset them, maybe provide them with a reason to consume and certainly ensure that nothing changes. As Marx suggested, capitalism loves a limit to overcome.

We need, instead, to start going to the media with the kind of consumables that will make them choke: 'We have to reclaim farce, produce and invent delirious subjectivities capable of clashing with capitalist subjectivity and make it crumble' (Guattari and Rolnik 2008, 42). As mentioned in the 'news' chapter, WikiLeaks has made precisely this move by producing a flow of information that the state cannot swallow or digest; which thus forces a real deterritorialisation of the state, constructing a line of flight toward humanity and liberty beyond the interests of the state and capital. Television news shows that satirise their own genre, such as the now defunct *Daily Show with Jon Stewart* and *The Colbert Report*, highlight the ludicrousness of not just their content but also their form, encouraging the viewer to accept the farcical nature of the media assemblage as part of their condition. While the true subversive potential of such programming is limited by its operation within the mass media assemblage, it reveals the insanity of that assemblage instead of simply denouncing it (Guattari and Rolnik 2008). Stewart and Colbert did not bring down the system and it has moved them both along now, but they will hopefully continue to produce fissures, farces and flow-disruptions. One day such a fissure will reach the right audience and create 'a-signifying rupture' that will release a flow over the whole social field and destroy the consumption-based, Oedipalising mass media assemblage entirely – blow it apart so we can create something new.

The second task of schizoanalysis is a more positive one – it is to map the flows of our desire; it is to become a mechanic, as Deleuze and Guattari repeatedly state – a tinkerer; it is to try to understand the machine that produces a particular effect, to understand its components and, more importantly, the organisation amongst those components: the abstract machine; it is to try to understand why it is that we want the world we have, to locate the desires that construct and flow through every assemblage. An example of applying this task to media is to think about social media and, particularly, the success of platforms such as Facebook. It is clear that Facebook launched its massive success on the back of understanding a particular desire. On the most fundamental level, this is the desire to connect, to make connections that could become productive of other things. This desire in itself is pure – a pure instance of desiring-production. However, by mapping what Facebook does with this desire, we can see how the desire is contorted in the assemblage. In the first instance, as described in the chapter on images, it presents your subjectivity as a series of faces and identifies you as an individual, and places each and every one such individual at the centre of their 'network' – everyone on Facebook has his or her own, unique, centre. Already you are thereby constructed as separate from the community, an object of distributed consumption. A stunning profile picture is used to generate exclusive connections – I am beautiful, I live a perfect life – which insinuates the lack in yours. Such a structure reterritorialises the capitalist subjectivity: I don't want to meet with you, I don't want to connect with you, I want to compete with you and win. At the same time Facebook turns your desire into a map of its own, a sophisticated map of desire registered through social graphs, interactions and page views. Instead of sharing this information, forcing a becoming-public of desire, it feeds the map straight back into the marketing assemblage, to use desire to generate more consumption, more profit.

Which brings us to the third task of schizoanalysis – to think about our assemblages of desire in terms of what they produce. Once we've mapped our desire, can we see how we can introduce a break-flow, an interruption, a line of flight or new connection that can make our desire work for us instead of against us? Can we make the machine, our machines, produce differently? Every investment of our desire has a social and ecological effect and we need to carefully assess that effect through its products. We cannot assess these effects through their representations, or through forming 'interest groups' to represent our interests to power. Instead, we must look directly at the products of desire and intervene at the level of the assemblage. We should not be constrained by what we think is sacrosanct – ideas such as the individual, family and the state have been imposed on desire, they did not precede it – and work to contain it. To refuse to think differently about such institutions is to invest in the paranoid, fascistic and reactionary pole of desire, instead of the schizoid, liberatory and revolutionary pole (Savat and Thompson 2015, 283–7). In media, this aspect of schizoanalysis should be pursued by tinkering with the media machines that we have – be they structures like the internet or structures like genre – and proliferating their connections, allowing them to become-rhizome so that we might liberate desire from its transcendental straightjacket and reintroduce it to the immanent, the local and the particular.

In short, a schizoanalysis of media should be asking questions that demand changes. Why, for instance, is Facebook a global phenomenon, while Ushahidi – a social networking platform for political protest and disaster relief – remains relatively unknown? Why, when global warming presents the most profound challenge to our species, does our information media treat it as a side issue only relevant to special interest groups? Why, given the regimes of violence propagated everywhere in the name of the flow of capital, do we look to media representations as the cause of that violence, rather than the symptom? All answers to this question implicate the profusion of an assemblage that prioritises the constructed individual and their 'interpellated interests' over the lived, immanent and real experiences and relations they produce (Faucher 2010, 58). The answers also implicate the role of media in constructing and maintaining that assemblage. This is precisely why Guattari advocated for a transition to a post-media age: 'What is terrifying' states Guattari, 'is the lack of collective imagination in a world that has reached such a boiling point' (Guattari 2009). As Guattari suggests, 'utopia today is to believe that current societies will be able to continue along on their merry little way [...] who would like for this "to hold up all the same," to return to yesterday and the day before yesterday' (Guattari 2009, 307). This, however, does not leave us in a position of cynicism, where we abandon all narratives in the manner of Lyotard, Baudrillard and others. Those positions stem precisely from an older image of thought, some of whose branches construct the social and political as traps, false copies, only poor resemblances of some world lost. Society cannot be reduced to such signifying chains. Instead what is needed is creativity, which is at the heart of Deleuze and Guattari's schizoanalysis.

Of course, schizoanalysis is not something you can prescribe. It is not a method but a meta-model (Guattari 1998) and what it requires will change according to the situation, but it is certainly something you can practise. 'The tools of schizoanalysis are inconsistent and continually evolving, arising, as they must, from their unique social and historical conditions' (Herzog 2008, 64). What Deleuze and Guattari are suggesting we do is to schizoanalyse the systems that our desire has created – trace its flows, seek to uncover how its energy is invested in producing this particular society – consider what our desire produces and then take that desire and reinvest in something new, something creative and something that will help people desire a new and better world.

NOTES

Introduction

1 See Buchanan (2015) for a discussion on why the term 'arrangement' may be more appropriate than the term 'assemblage'.

Assemblages

1 Deleuze attributes this idea to David Hume (Deleuze 1991).

Play and games

1 Deleuze and Guattari's description of the legitimate and illegitimate uses of the syntheses takes place in Anti-Oedipus (2004a, 1–54); the following summary of their argument benefits largely from their explanation in Buchanan (2000, 24–6) and Holland (2012, 322–6).

2 Ian Bogost has covered this practice extensively in his work on gamification. See Bogost (2011).

3 These examples are more thoroughly explored in Harper (2009b) and McGonigal (2011).

News and information media

1 For a full account of the BwO and how it relates to Artaud's thinking, see the 'body without organs' entry in Buchanan (2010).

2 Hegel and Plato are two examples of examples to which Deleuze consistently refers in this context.

3 We should remind our readers that this new distribution machine is not a function of the printed book and printing press as such, but rather an expression of the society that produced the printing press.

4 Etymologically, 'news' evolved from the plural of new ... news.

5 Indeed, it is in precisely this way that Deleuze and Guattari argue the socius is maintained in the face of the destructive, deterritorialising force of capitalism.

6 Herman and Chomsky advanced the argument in Chomsky and Herman 1988 and their model has been debated and amended ad nauseam. For a recent instance see Mullen and Klaehn (2010).

7 The legacy of these actions are the 'open library' and 'recap' systems, which continue to facilitate this free access.

8 For a fuller exploration of the military–industrial–media– entertainment assemblage see Der Derian (2001).

Advertising

1 Deleuze and Guattari only really used the term 'desiring-production' at the time of writing *Anti-Oedipus* (1972), clearly with the intent of ensuring there was no confusion about their concept of desire and that of Freud and Lacan. However, from the publication of their book on Kafka (Deleuze and Guattari 1986), they consistently drop 'production', and simply use 'desire' in the same positive and productive sense.

2 As noted elsewhere (Harper 2009b), being goal oriented seems to be the worst possible form of foreplay.

3 Manson refers to the brand names Acura and Colgate at this point.

4 An old joke mentions that while Freud's father was unpleasant, his mother was particularly attractive.

5 Nancy Fraser (1992), among others, has usefully pointed out that more marginalised public spheres were often dominated by women, who conducted their own, almost clandestine series of coding of flows.

6 The rise of brands in the nineties was in some sense an early precursor of this new marketing strategy, as it was a strategy to deliver a consistent and powerful message in the face of the proliferation of channels and platforms (Klein 2000).

7   This idea is explored far more earnestly and optimistically by Eugene Holland (2011).

8   For a summary of these arguments, see Negroponte (1995, 164–5) and Savat (2013, 50–7) respectively.

Media content and audiences

1   The term gender has the same etymological root as genre, generic, genesis and generate – 'gene'.

2   This quote appears within a broader attack on Hegelian dialectics as a way of understanding and employing difference.

3   For a more comprehensive account of how art, immanence and 'the new' relate to each other in Deleuze's thought see Sholtz (2015).

4   A full exploration of live performance in the age of digital technology, and how it relates to the experience of jouissance, can be found in Harper (2015).

BIBLIOGRAPHY

Adorno, Theodor W. 2002. *Essays on Music*, translated by Susan
H. Gillespie, ed. Richard Leppert. Los Angeles, CA: University of
California Press.

Adorno, Theodor and Max Horkheimer. 1997. *The Dialectics of
Enlightenment*. London: Verso. Original edition, 1944.

Angel, Maria and Anna Gibbs. 2006. 'Media, Affect and the
Face: Biomediation and the Political Scene.' *Southern Review:
Communication, Politics and Culture* 38 (2): 24–39.

Ansell-Pearson, Keith. 2005. 'The Reality of the Virtual: Bergson and
Deleuze.' *MLN* 120 (5): 1112–27.

Arendt, Hannah. 1958. *The Human Condition*. Chicago: University of
Chicago Press.

Aristotle. 1999. *Politics*, translated by Benjamin Jowett. Kitchener,
Ontario, Batoche Books.

Artaud, Antonin. 1976. 'To Have Done with the Judgment of God.'
In *Selected Writings*, translated by Helen Weaver, edited by Susan
Sontag. Berkley, CA: University of California Press.

Batchelor, James. 2014. '18 Things we Learned about *Alien: Isolation
Last Night*.' Develop. http://www.develop-online.net/analysis/18-
things-we-learned-about-alien-isolation-last-night/0189188 (accessed
23 February 2016).

Baudrillard, Jean. 1994. *Simulacra and Simulation*, translated by Sheila
Faria Glaser. Ann Arbor: University of Michigan Press.

Beckman, Frida. 2013. *Between Desire and Pleasure: A Deleuzean
Theory of Sexuality*. Edinburgh: Edinburgh University Press.

Bell, Jeffrey A. 2012. 'Modes of Violence: Deleuze, Whitehead, Butler
and the Challenge of Dialogue.' In *Butler on Whitehead: On the
Occasion*, translated by Harry Zohn, 127–43. Lanham, MD:
Lexington Books.

Benjamin, Walter. 1969. 'The Work of Art in the Age of Mechanical
Reproduction', edited by Roland Faber, Michael Halewood, Deena
Lin. In *Illuminations*, edited by Hannah Arendt, 217–51. New York:
Schocken Books.

Black, Michaela, Darryl Charles, Ben Cowley and Ray Hickey. 2008.

'Toward an Understanding of Flow in Video Games.' *Computers in Entertainment* 6 (2): 1–27. doi: 10.1145/1371216.1371223.

Bogost, Ian. 2011. 'Persuasive Games: Exploitationware.' *Gamasutra*. Accessed 23 February 2016.

Bogue, Ronald. 2007. *Deleuze's Way: Essays in Transverse Ethics and Aesthetics*. Aldershot: Ashgate.

Bolter, Jay David and Richard Grusin. 2000. *Remediation: Understanding New Media*. Boston, MA: MIT Press.

boyd, danah. 2010. 'Social Network Sites as Networked Publics: Affordances, Dynamics, and Implications.' In *Networked Self: Identity, Community, and Culture on Social Network Sites*, edited by Z. Papacharissi, 39–58. New York: Routledge.

boyd, danah and N. B. Ellison. 2007. 'Social Network Sites: Definition, History and Scholarship.' *Journal of Computer Mediated Communication* 13 (1): 210–30.

Bruns, Axel. 2003. 'Gatewatching, Not Gatekeeping: Collaborative Online News.' *Media International Australia Incorporating Culture and Policy: Quarterly Journal of Media Research and Resources* 107: 31–44.

Buchanan, Ian. 1997. 'Deleuze and Pop Music.' *Australian Humanities Review* (7): 1–5.

Buchanan, Ian. 2000. *Deleuzism*. Durham, NC: Duke University Press.

Buchanan, Ian. 2008. *Deleuze and Guattari's Anti-Oedipus: A Reader's Guide*. London: Continuum.

Buchanan, Ian. 2009. 'Deleuze and the Internet.' In *Deleuze and New Technology*, edited by Mark Poster and David Savat, 143–60. Edinburgh: Edinburgh University Press.

Buchanan, Ian. 2010. *A Dictionary of Critical Theory*. Oxford: Oxford University Press.

Buchanan, Ian. 2015. 'Assemblage Theory and its Discontents.' *Deleuze. Guattari. Schizoanalysis. Education: Deleuze Studies*, edited by Greg Thompson and David Savat 9 (3): 382–93.

Byrne, David. 1993. Angels. In *Angels*. Los Angeles: Luaka Bop/Warner Bros.

Caillois, R. 2001. *Man, Play, and Games*, translated by Meyer Barash. Champaign: University of Illinois Press.

Castaneda, Carlos. 1971. *The Teachings of Don Juan*. Berkeley: University of California Press.

Castronova, Edward. 2007. *Exodus to the Virtual World: How Online Fun is Changing Reality*. Basingstoke: Palgrave Macmillan.

Chomsky, Noam. 2003. *Hegemony or Survival: America's Quest for Global Dominance*. Sydney: Allen & Unwin.

Chomsky, Noam and Edward S. Herman. 1988. *Manufacturing Consent:*

The Political Economy of the Mass Media. New York: Pantheon Books.

Colman, Felicity J. 2005. 'Affect.' In *The Deleuze Dictionary,* edited by Adrian Parr, 11–14. Edinburgh: Edinburgh University Press.

Colman, Felicity J. 2012. 'Play as an Affective Field for Activating Subjectivity: Notes on *The Machinic Unconscious.' Deleuze Studies* 6 (2): 250–64.

Cook, Ian. 2009. 'The Body without Organs and Internet Gaming Adiction.' In *Deleuze and New Technology,* edited by Mark Poster and David Savat. Edinburgh: Edinburgh University Press.

Crandall, J. 2010. 'The Geospatialisation of Calculative Operations Tracking, Sensing and Megacities.' *Theory, Culture & Society* 27 (6): 68–90.

Cremin, Colin. 2012. 'The Formal Qualities of the Video Game: An Exploration of *Super Mario Galaxy* with Gilles Deleuze.' *Games and Culture* 7 (1): 72–86.

Cremin, Colin. 2015. *Exploring Videogames with Deleuze and Guattari: Towards an Affective Theory of Form.* Oxford: Routledge.

Csikszentmihalyi, Mihaly. 1990. *Flow, the Psychology of Optimal Experience.* New York: Harper Perennial.

Csikszentmihalyi, Mihaly. 2004. 'Mihaly Csikszentmihalyi: Flow, the Secret to Happiness.' TED Talk.

Day, Felicia. 2014. 'The Only Thing I Have to Say about Gamer Gate.' http://thisfeliciaday.tumblr.com/post/100700417809/the-only-thingi-have-to-say-about-gamer-gate (accessed 11 September 2015).

Dayan, Daniel and Elihu Katz. 1994. *Media Events.* Cambridge, MA: Harvard University Press.

Deleuze, Gilles. 1986. *Cinema 1: The Movement-Image,* translated by Hugh Tomlinson and Barbara Habberjam. Minneapolis: University of Minnesota Press.

Deleuze, Gilles. 1989. *Cinema 2: The Time Image,* translated by Hugh Tomlinson and Robert Galeta. Minneapolis: University of Minnesota Press.

Deleuze, Gilles. 1953 (1991). *Empiricism and Subjectivity: An Essay on Hume's Theory of Human Nature,* translated by Constantin Boundas, New York: Columbia University Press.

Deleuze, Gilles. 1992. 'Postscript on Societies of Control.' *October* 59: 3–7.

Deleuze, Gilles. 1994. *Difference and Repetition,* translated by Paul Patton. New York: Columbia University Press.

Deleuze, Gilles. 1995. *Negotiations,* translated by Martin Joughin. New York: Columbia University Press.

Deleuze, Gilles. 1998. 'Having an Idea in Cinema (On the Cinema of Straub-Huillet),' translated by Eleanor Kaufman. In *Deleuze and Guattari: New Mappings in Politics, Philosophy and Culture*, edited by Eleanor Kaufman and Kevin Jon Heller. Minneapolis: University of Minnesota Press.

Deleuze, Gilles. 2000. 'The Brain is the Screen: An Interview with Gilles Deleuze,' translated by Marie Therese Guirgis. In *The Brain is the Screen: Deleuze and the Philosophy of Cinema*, edited by Gregory Flaxman. Minneapolis: University of Minnesota Press.

Deleuze, Gilles. 2001. 'Dualism, Monism and Multiplicities,' translated by Daniel W. Smith. *Contretemps* 2: 92–108 (May).

Deleuze, Gilles. 2003. *Francis Bacon: The Logic of Sensation*, translated by Daniel W. Smith. London: Continuum.

Deleuze, Gilles. 2004a. *Desert Islands*, translated by Mike Taormina. Los Angeles, CA: Semiotext(e).

Deleuze, Gilles. 2004b. *Difference and Repetition*, translated by Paul Patton. London: Continuum.

Deleuze, Gilles. 2004c. 'Three Group Related Problems.' In *Desert Islands and Other Texts*, translated by Michael Taormina, edited by David Lapoujade, 193–203. Los Angeles, CA: Semiotext(e).

Deleuze, Gilles. 2005. *Expressionism in Philosophy: Spinoza*, translated by Martin Joughin. New York: Zone Books. Original edition, 1968.

Deleuze, Gilles. 2006. *Nietzsche and Philosophy*, translated by Hugh Tomlinson. New York: Columbia University Press.

Deleuze, Gilles. 2007. *Two Regimes of Madness: Texts and Interviews 1975–1995*, translated by Ames Hodges and Mike Taormina, edited by David Lapoujade. New York: Semoitext(e).

Deleuze, Gilles. 2008. *Proust and Signs: The Complete Test*, translated by Richard Howard. London: Continuum.

Deleuze, Gilles and Félix Guattari. 1983. *Anti-Oedipus: Capitalism and Schizophrenia*, translated by Robert Hurley, Mark Seem, Helen R. Lane. Minneapolis: University of Minnesota Press.

Deleuze, Gilles and Félix Guattari. 1986. *Kafka: Towards a Minor Literature*, translated by Dana Polan. Minneapolis: University of Minnesota Press.

Deleuze, Gilles and Félix Guattari. 1987. *A Thousand Plateaus: Capitalism and Schizophrenia*, translated by B. Massumi. Minneapolis: University of Minnesota Press.

Deleuze, Gilles and Félix Guattari. 1994. *What is Philosophy?*, translated by Hugh Tomlinson and Graham Burchell. New York: Columbia University Press.

Deleuze, Gilles and Félix Guattari. 2004a. *Anti-Oedipus: Capitalism and Schizophrenia*, translated by Robert Hurley, Mark Seem, Helen R. Lane. London: Continuum.

Deleuze, Gilles and Félix Guattari. 2004b. *A Thousand Plateaus*, translated by Brian Massumi. London: Continuum.

Deleuze, Gilles and C. Parnet. 2012. *From A to Z*, directed by Pierre-André Boutang, translated by Charles J. Stivale. Los Angeles: Semiotext(e).

Der Derian, James. 2001. *Virtuous War: Mapping the Military–Industrial–Media–Entertainment Network*. Boulder, CO: Westview Press.

Edson, C. Jr. 2015. 'Journalism is Twerking?: How Web Analytics is changing the Process of Gatekeeping.' *New Media and Society* 16 (4): 559–75.

Eisenstein, Elizabeth. 1979. *The Printing Press as an Agent of Change: Communications and Cultural Transformations in Early Modern Europe*. London: Cambridge University Press.

Elliot, Paul. 2012. *Guattari Reframed*. London: I. B. Taurus.

Ewen, Stuart. 1976. *Captains of Consciousness*: New York: McGraw-Hill.

Faucher, Kane X. 2010. 'McDeleuze: What's More Rhizomal Than a Big Mac?' *Deleuze Studies* 4 (1): 42–59.

Flaxman, Gregory and Elena Oxman. 2008. 'Losing Face.' In *Deleuze and the Schizoanalysis of Cinema*, edited by Ian Buchanan and Patricia MacCormack. Edinburgh: Edinburgh University Press.

Fraser, Nancy. 1992. 'Rethinking the Public Sphere: A Contribution to the Critique of Actually Existing Democracy.' In *Habermas and the Public Sphere*, edited by Craig Calhoun. Cambridge, MA: MIT Press.

Gaffney, Peter. 2010. *The Force of the Virtual: Deleuze, Science and Philosophy*. Minnesota: University of Minnesota Press.

Galloway, A. R. 2006. *Gaming: Essays on Algorithmic Culture*. Minnesota: University of Minnesota Press.

Genosko, Gary. 2012. 'Guattari TV, By Kafka.' *Deleuze Studies* 6 (2): 210–23.

Gibson, William and Rosenberg, Scott. 2014. 'The Man Who Named Cyberspace.' In *Conversations with William Gibson*, edited by Patrick A. Smith. Jackson: University Press of Mississippi.

Gledhill, Christine. 2000. 'Genre.' In *Reinventing Film Studies*, edited by Christine Gledhill and Linda Williams, 221–43. London: Edward Arnold.

Graeber, David. 2015. *The Utopia of Rules: On Technology, Stupidity, and the Secret Joys of Bureaucracy*. Brooklyn: Melville House Publishing.

Green, Joshua and Henry Jenkins. 2011. 'Spreadable Media: How Audiences Create Value and Meaning in a Networked Economy.' In *The Handbook of Media Audiences*, edited by Virginia Nightingale, 109–27. New York: John Wiley & Sons.

Guattari, Félix. 1989. 'The Three Ecologies.' *New Formations*, translated by Chris Turner 8: 131–47.

Guattari, Félix. 1993. 'Machinic Heterogenesis.' In *Rethinking Technologies*, edited by V. A. Conley, translated by Iames Creech. Minneapolis: University of Minnesota Press.

Guattari, Félix. 1995. *Chaosmosis: An ethico-aesthetic paradigm*, translated by Paul Bains and Julian Pefanis. Bloomington: Indiana University Press.

Guattari, Félix. 2009. *Soft Subversions: Texts and Interviews 1977–1985*, translated by Chet Wiener and Emily Wittman. Los Angeles, CA: Semiotext(e).

Guattari, Félix. 2011a. *The Machinic Unconscious: Essays in Schizoanalysis*, translated by Taylor Adkins. Los Angeles: Semiotext(e).

Guattari, Félix. 2011b. 'On Contemporary Art: Interview with Oliver Zahm, April 1992.' In *The Guattari Effect*, edited by Éric Alliez and Andrew Goffey, translated by Stephen Zepke. 40–56. London: Continuum.

Guattari, Félix and Suely Rolnik. 2008. *Molecular Revolution in Brazil*, translated by Karel Clapshow and Brian Holmes. Los Angeles, CA: Semiotext(e).

Guattari, Félix. 1998. 'Schizoanalysis.' *The Yale Journal of Criticism*, translated by Mohamed Zayani 11 (2): 433–9.

Habermas, Jürgen. 1979. *Communication and the Evolution of Society*, translated by Thomas McCarthy. Boston, MA: Beacon Press.

Habermas, Jürgen. 1987. *The Theory of Communicative Action: Lifeworld and System – A Critique of Functionalist Reason*, translated by T. McCarthy, Vol. 2. Boston MA: Beacon Press.

Habermas, Jürgen. 1989. *The Structural Transformation of the Public Sphere: An Inquiry into a Category of Bourgeois Society*, translated by Thomas Burger. Cambridge: MIT Press. Original edition, 1962.

Hallinan, Blake and Ted Striphas. 2014. 'Recommended for You: The Netflix Prize and the Production of Algorithmic Culture.' *New Media and Society* 23 June: 1–21.

Harper, Tauel. 2009a. 'Smash the Strata! A Program for Techno-Political (r)Evolution.' In *Deleuze and New Technology*, edited by Mark Poster and David Savat. Edinburgh: Edinburgh University Press.

Harper, Tauel. 2009b. 'The Smooth Spaces of Play: Deleuze and the Emancipatory Potential of Games.' *Symploke* 17 (1–2): 129–2.

Harper, Tauel. 2011. *Democracy in the Age of New Media: The Politics of the Spectacle*. New York: Peter Lang.

Harper, Tauel. 2015. 'Aura, Iteration and Action: Digital Technology and the Jouissance of Live Music.' In *The Digital Evolution of Live Music*, edited by Angela Cresswell Jones and Rebecca Jane Bennett. Oxford: Chandos.

Herman, Edward S. and Robert W. McChesney. 2001. *The Global Media: The New Missionaries of Corporate Capitalism.* London: Continuum.

Herzog, Amy. 2008. 'Suspended Gestures: Schizoanalysis, Affect and the Face in Cinema.' In *Deleuze and the Schizoanalysis of Cinema*, edited by Ian Buchanan and Patricia MacCormack, 63–74. London: Continuum.

Holland, Eugene. 2011. *Nomad Citizenship: Free Market Communism and the Slow Motion General Strike.* Minneapolis: Minnesota University Press.

Holland, Eugene. 2012. 'Deleuze and Pyschoanalysis.' In *Cambridge Companion to Deleuze*, edited by Daniel W. Smith and Henry Sommers-Hall. Cambridge: Cambridge University Press.

Hughes, Joe. 2009. *Deleuze's Difference and Repetition.* London: Continuum.

Hughes, Joe. 2012. *Philosophy After Deleuze.* Bloomsbury: New York.

Huizinga, Johan. 1948. *Homo Ludens: A Study of the Play-Element in Culture*, translated by R. F. C. Hull. London: Routledge & Kegan Paul.

Iyengar, Shanto. 1990. 'Framing Responsibility for Political Issues.' *Political Behaviour* 12 (1): 19–40.

Kafka, Franz. 2008. *The Complete Novels of Kafka*, translated by Willa and Edwin Muir. London: Vintage Classics.

Kandel. 2006. *In Search of Memory: The Emergence of a New Science of Mind.* New York: Newton.

Klein, Naomi. 2000. *No Logo.* New York: Picador.

Knorr-Cetina, K. 2007. 'Global Markets as Global Conversations.' *Text & Talk* 27 (5–6): 705–34.

Knorr Cetina, Karin and Alex Preda. 2007. 'The Temporalization of Financial Markets: From Network to Flow.' *Theory, Culture & Society* 24: 116–38.

Leaver, Tama and Michele Willson. 2015. 'Zynga's Farmville, Social Games and the Ethics of Big Data Mining.' *Communication Research and Practice* 1 (2).

Lenderman, Max. 2006. *Experience the Message: How Experiential Marketing is Changing the Brand World.* New York: Carrol & Graf.

Lessig, Lawrence. 2008. *Remix: Making Art and Commerce Thrive in the Hybrid Economy.* London: Bloomsbury.

Levine, Michael P. 2015. 'Witnessing Katrina: Morbid Curiosity and the Aesthetics of Disaster.' In *The 'Katrina Effect': On the Nature of the Catastrophe*, edited by William M. Taylor, Michael P Levine, Oenone Rooksby and Joely-Kym Sobott. London: Bloomsbury.

Lucas, George. 1977. Star Wars [Film]. 20th Century Fox.

Madrigal, Alexis C. 2014. 'How Netflix Reverse Engineered Hollywood.' *The Atlantic*, 2 January.

Maras, Steven. 2000. 'One of Many Media.' *M/C* 3 (6).

Marcuse, Herbert. 1964. *One Dimensional Man: Studies in the Ideology of Advanced Industrial Society*, 2nd ed. Boston: Beacon Press. Reprint, 1991.

Marx, Karl. 1973. *Grundrisse*, translated by Martin Nicolaus. New York: Vintage.

Massumi, Brian. 2009. 'National Enterprise Emergency: Steps Toward an Ecology of Powers.' *Theory, Culture & Society* 26 (6): 153–85.

McGonigal, Jane. 2011. *Reality is Broken: Why Games Make Us Better and How They Can Change the World*. London: Random House.

McLuhan, Marshall. 1964. *Understanding Media: The Extensions of Man*. New York: McGraw-Hill.

Monaco, James. 2009. *How to Read a Film*. Oxford: Oxford University Press.

Moore, Michael. 2002. *Bowling for Columbine* [Film], USA: MGM.

Morozov, Evgeny. 2015. 'Google May Have Changed its Name but the Game Remains the Same.' *The Guardian*, Sunday 16 August. http://www.theguardian.com/commentisfree/2015/aug/16/google-alphabet-name-change-same-game-evgeny-morozov (accessed 19 September 2015).

Morse, Margaret. 1998. *Virtualities: Television, Media Art and Cyberculture*. Bloomington: Indiana University Press.

Mullen, Andrew and Jeffrey Klaehn. 2010. 'The Herman-Chomsky Propaganda Model: A Critical Approach to Analysing Mass Media Behaviour.' *Sociology Compass* 4 (4): 215–29.

Mumford, Lewis. 1995. 'The Monastery and the Clock.' In *The Lewis Mumford Reader*, edited by D. L. Miller. Athens: University of Georgia Press.

Negroponte, Nicholas. 1995. *Being Digital*. Rydalmere, N.S.W.: Hodder & Stoughton.

Ong, Walter J. 2000. *Orality and Literacy: The Technologizing of the Word*. London: Routledge.

Pariser, Eli. 2011. *The Filter Bubble: How the New Personalized Web is Changing What We Read and How We Think*. New York: Penguin Books.

Perry, Colton and Tyrone Anderson. 2013. *Hitting a Personalization Home Run with Data*. London: Monetate. http://fast.wistia.net/embed/iframe/srlkxmu8e3?autoPlay=true&controlsVisibleOnLoad=true&endVideoBehaviour=reset&popover=true&version=v1&videoHeight=360&videoWidth=640 (accessed 3 April 2015).

Pisters, Patricia. 2006. 'Arresting the Flux of Images and Sounds: Free Indirect Discourse and the Dialectics of Political Cinema.' In *Deleuze and the Contemporary World*, edited by Ian Buchanan and Adrian Parr. Edinburgh: Edinburgh University Press.

PornHub. 2015. '2014 Year in Review'. http://www.pornhub.com/ insights/2014-year-in-review (accessed 28 August 2015).

Poster, Mark. 2001. *What's the Matter with the Internet?* Minneapolis: Minnesota University Press.

Postman, Neil. 1985. *Amusing Ourselves to Death: Public Discourse in the Age of Show Business*. USA: Penguin.

Powell, Anna. 2002. 'Kicking the Map Away: The Blair Witch Project, Deleuze and the Aesthetics of Horror.' *Spectator* 22 (2): 56–68.

Radiohead. 1997. Fitter Happier. *OK Computer*. London: Parlophone Capitol.

Rizzo, Terresa. 2012. *Deleuze and Film: A Feminist Introduction.* London: Bloomsbury.

Romanyshyn, Robert Donald. 1989. *Technology as Symptom and Dream*. London: Routledge.

Rudder, Christian. 2014. *Dataclysm: Who We Are (When We Think No One's Looking)*. New York: Crown Publishing.

Rushton, Richard. 2002. 'What Can a Face Do? On Deleuze and Faces.' *Cultural Critique* 51: 219–37.

Savat, David. 2013. *Uncoding the Digital: Technology, Subjectivity and Action in the Control Society*. London: Palgrave Macmillan.

Savat, David and Greg Thompson. 2015. 'Education and the Relation to the Outside: A Little Real Reality.' *Deleuze. Guattari. Schizoanalysis. Education: Deleuze Studies*, edited by Greg Thompson and David Savat 9 (3): 273–300.

Schivelbusch, W. 1986. *The Railway Journey: The Industrialization of Time and Space in the 19th Century*. Leamington Spa: Berg.

Shaviro, Steven. 1993. *The Cinematic Body*. Minneapolis: University of Minnesota Press.

Sheffield, Brandon. 2013. 'Opinion: Let's Retire the Word "Gamer".' *Gamasutra.* http://www.gamasutra.com/view/news/192107/Opinion Lets retire the word gamer.php (accessed 11 November 2015).

Sholtz, Janae. 2015. *The Invention of a People: Heidegger and Deleuze on Art and the Political*. Edinburgh: Edinburgh University Press.

Shouse, Eric. 2005. 'Feeling, Emotion, Affect.' *M/C* 8 (6).

Smith, Daniel W. 2011. 'Flow, Code and Stock: A Note on Deleuze's Political Philosophy.' *Deleuze Studies* 5 (supplement) (1–6): 36–55.

Smith, Daniel W. 2012. *Essays on Deleuze*. Edinburgh: Edinburgh University Press.

Smith, David. 2015. 'Google Chairman: "The Internet Will Disappear".' *Business Insider Australia*, January 27. http://www.businessinsider.

com.au/google-chief-eric-schmidt-the-internet-will-disappear-2015-1 (accessed 19 September 2015).

Smith, Robert James, Andrew Laurence Tolhurst and Simon Gallup. 1981. Primary. In *Faith*. Fiction Records, Polydor.

Strogatz, S. 2012. *The Joy of X*: Boston: Houghton Mifflin Harcourt.

Sutton-Smith, Brian. 2006. 'Play and Ambiguity.' In *The Game Design Reader: A Rules of Play Anthology*, edited by Katie Salen and Eric Zimmerman. Cambridge, MA: MIT Press.

Sweney, Mark. 2014. 'Netflix Gathers Detailed Viewer Data to Guide its Search for the Next Hit.' *The Guardian*, Monday 24 February. http://www.theguardian.com/media/2014/feb/23/netflix-viewer-data-house-of-cards (accessed 13 April 2015).

Talking Heads. 1984. *Stop Making Sense*. Burbank, CA: Sire/Warner Bros.

Theall, Donald F. 2001. *The Virtual Marshall McLuhan*. Montreal: McGill-Queens University Press.

Thompson, Greg and Ian Cook. 2013. 'Mapping Teacher-Faces.' *Studies in Philosophy and Education* 32 (4): 379–95.

Timm, Trevor. 2015. 'Iran DSupporters Have More Cred. But Opponents Have the Media-Savvy.' *The Guardian*, 12 August 2015. http://www.theguardian.com/commentisfree/2015/aug/12/iran-deal-supporters-credibility (accessed 19 September 2015).

Tomkinson, Sian and Tauel Harper. 2015. 'The Position of Women in Video Game Culture: The Perez and Day Twitter Incident.' *Continuum: Journal of Media & Cultural Studies* 29 (4): 617–34.

Tropes, TV. 2015. 'Inspirationally Disadvantaged.' Accessed 27 August 2015.

Tropes, TV. 2015. 'TV Tropes Will Ruin Your Life.' http://tvtropes.org/pmwiki/pmwiki.php/Main/TVTropesWillRuinYourLife (accessed 27 August 2015).

Tussey, Ethan. 2014. 'The Online Prime Time of Workspace Media.' In *Spreadable Media*, edited by Henry Jenkins, Sam Ford and Joshua Green. New York: New York University Press.

Ueno, Toshiya. 2012. 'Guattari and Japan.' *Deleuze Studies* 6 (2): 187–209.

Vedrashiko, Ilya. 2014. 'How Spreadability Changes How We Think About Advertising.' In *Spreadable Media*, edited by Henry Jenkins, Sam Ford and Joshua Green. New York: New York University Press.

Virilio, Paul. 1986. *Speed and Politics: An Essay on Dromology*, translated by M. Polizzoti. New York: Columbia University Press.

Wallin, Jason. 2012. 'Bon Mots for Bad Thoughts.' *Discourse: Studies in the Cultural Politics of Education* 33 (1): 147–62.

Watercutter, Angela. 2014. Bronies are Redefining Fandom – and American Manhood. *Wired* (3 November 2014). http://www.wired/com/2014/03/bronies-online-fandom/ (accessed 28 August 2015).

Williams, Raymond. 2003. *Television: Technology and Cultural Form.* London: Routledge.

Willson, Michele. 2015. 'Social Games as Partial Platforms for Identity Co-creation.' *Media International Australia* (154): 15–24.

Wolfsfeld, Gadi. 1997. *The Media and Political Conflict.* Cambridge: Cambridge University Press.

Woods, S. 2007. 'Playing With An Other: Ethics in the Magic Circle.' In *Cybertext Yearbook – Ludology,* edited by M. Eskelinen and G. Frasca. Jyvaskyla, Finland: University of Jyvaskyla.

Woods, Stewart John. 2009. '(Play) Ground Rules: The Social Conract and the Magic Circle.' *Observatio* (8): 204–22.

Zhang, Peter. 2011. 'Deleuze's Relay and Extension of McLuhan: An Ethical Exploration.' *Explorations in Media Ecology* 10 (3–4): 207–24.

Zizek, Slavoj. 1994. 'The Spectre of Ideology.' In *Mapping Ideology,* edited by Slavoj Zizek, 1–33. London: Verso.

INDEX